A Potter's Progress

A POTTER'S PROGRESS

Emanuel Suter and the Business of Craft

● ● ●

SCOTT HAMILTON SUTER

The University of Tennessee Press
KNOXVILLE

FRONTISPIECE: EMANUEL SUTER (1833–1902), 1895. COURTESY OF THE VIRGINIA
MENNONITE CONFERENCE ARCHIVE.

THE PAPER IN THIS BOOK MEETS THE REQUIREMENTS OF AMERICAN NATIONAL
STANDARDS INSTITUTE / NATIONAL INFORMATION STANDARDS ORGANIZATION
SPECIFICATION Z39.48–1992 (PERMANENCE OF PAPER). IT CONTAINS 30 PERCENT POST-
CONSUMER WASTE AND IS CERTIFIED BY THE FOREST STEWARDSHIP COUNCIL.

LIBRARY OF CONGRESS CATALOGING-IN-PUBLICATION DATA

NAMES: SUTER, SCOTT HAMILTON, AUTHOR.
TITLE: A POTTER'S PROGRESS : EMANUEL SUTER AND THE BUSINESS OF CRAFT /
   SCOTT HAMILTON SUTER.
DESCRIPTION: KNOXVILLE : THE UNIVERSITY OF TENNESSEE PRESS, 2020. |
   INCLUDES BIBLIOGRAPHICAL REFERENCES AND INDEX. | SUMMARY: "BORN INTO A
   TRADITIONAL, MENNONITE CULTURE IN 1833, EMANUEL SUTER CULTIVATED THE
   ART OF POTTERY AND EXPANDED MARKETS ACROSS THE SHENANDOAH VALLEY OF
   VIRGINIA, CREATING A THRIVING COMPANY AND LEAVING THOUSANDS OF EXAMPLES
   OF UTILITARIAN CERAMIC WARE THAT HAVE SURVIVED DOWN TO THE PRESENT.
   DRAWING ON THE POTTER'S DETAIL-RICH DIARY AND NUMEROUS PRIMARY AND
   SECONDARY SOURCES, SUTER'S GREAT-GREAT-GRANDSON SCOTT HAMILTON SUTER
   TELLS THE STORY OF HOW A FARMER WITH A SEASONAL SIDELINE BECAME A
   TECHNOLOGICALLY ADVANCED ENTREPRENEUR OPERATING A MODERN INDUSTRIAL
   COMPANY. ENHANCED BY OVER TWO DOZEN COLOR IMAGES AND AN EXAMINATION
   OF DAILY LIFE IN SUTER'S SHOPS, THIS VIVID CASE STUDY SHOWS HOW ONE
   CRAFTSMAN'S UNCOMMON CAREER PATH BECAME A TEMPLATE FOR PROGRESS IN LATE
   NINETEENTH-CENTURY AMERICA—A SIGN OF THE MARKET ECONOMY TO COME."—
   PROVIDED BY PUBLISHER.
IDENTIFIERS: LCCN 2019036772 (PRINT) | LCCN 2019036773 (EBOOK) |
   ISBN 9781621905257 (HARDCOVER) | ISBN 9781621905370 (PDF)
SUBJECTS: LCSH: SUTER, EMANUEL, 1833–1902. | POTTERS—SHENANDOAH RIVER
   VALLEY (VA. AND W. VA.)—BIOGRAPHY. | POTTERY INDUSTRY—SHENANDOAH RIVER
   VALLEY (VA. AND W. VA.)—HISTORY—19TH CENTURY.
CLASSIFICATION: LCC HD9611.95.S88 S87 2020 (PRINT) | LCC HD9611.95.S88
   (EBOOK) | DDC 338.4/7738092 [B]—DC23
LC RECORD AVAILABLE AT HTTPS://LCCN.LOC.GOV/2019036772
LC EBOOK RECORD AVAILABLE AT HTTPS://LCCN.LOC.GOV/2019036773

Dedicated to my parents

CONTENTS

ILLUSTRATIONS

(Following page 104)

ACKNOWLEDGMENTS

From an early age I was familiar with the pottery of my great-great-grandfather Emanuel Suter, although like most younger folks I hadn't given too much thought to ancestors and how they lived. Only when I sat in Terry Zug's classroom at the University of North Carolina–Chapel Hill in 1986 did I begin to fully understand the significance of my forebear's occupation. At Terry's urging I first began to explore Emanuel Suter's work that year, and I continue to research his motivations and products to this day. This manuscript is the result of those many years of investigation, and it would not have come to fruition without the support of many friends, family members, colleagues, and institutions.

I received valuable advice and guidance in the nascent stages of this research from John Vlach, my mentor during my years of study at the George Washington University. His enthusiasm and insights into material folk culture molded my thinking on many topics related to this book. Similarly, Bernard Mergen introduced me to the key role that material culture studies play in understanding any culture. His thoughtful observations on applying this methodology to Emanuel Suter's work are also evident throughout this effort.

The librarians and archivists at Eastern Mennonite University have always been helpful, kind, and understanding, and have provided much support for this project for many years. Lois Bowman Kreider and Harold Huber spent many hours responding to my research requests and offered helpful comments on Mennonite history and culture. Simone Horst, special collections librarian, has also supported this research in many ways.

Many conversations with other long-time researchers of Shenandoah Valley culture have contributed to my thoughts on Suter's life and work. Collaborations with Jeffrey Evans have been fruitful over the years, and I thank him for continuing to provide information from his own research into the Shenandoah Valley pottery tradition. Similarly, Cheryl Lyon and Dale Harter, expert Shenandoah Valley scholars, have provided research help and advice for many years. I am also grateful to William McGuffin, who applied his photography skills to the pottery featured in the book. The manuscript benefitted from comments provided by Betsy White, Mark Sawin, and an anonymous reviewer. Their observations made this a more complete work. I am also grateful to Scot Danforth at the University of Tennessee Press for encouraging me to persevere with this project.

I am also indebted to the many collectors of both pottery and manuscripts and to others who spend time thinking about the significance of traditional pottery and Shenandoah Valley culture for assisting me in many ways: Lindsay Bloch; Kent Botkin; Jeff Bradfield; Betty Suter Feldman; Brenda Hornsby Heindl; Michael Hough; Robert Hunter; Robert Jolley; Stan Kaufman; Richard Martin, Donald Miller; Steven Miller; Cameron Nickels; Kurt Russ; Sarah Suter Splaun; Elizabeth and Frank Suter; Marcia and Tom Suter; Norma and Stanley Suter; and Rudy Tucker. Each of these folks have offered advice, observations, research, or access to their collections.

Bridgewater College has supported my research on this project with a sabbatical leave and faculty research grants that enabled substantial work to be completed. The Margaret Grattan Weaver Institute for Regional Culture at Bridgewater College also provided important funding for the completion of this project.

Finally, I thank my family for their patience and encouragement throughout the years that I have looked into the life and work of Emanuel Suter. I am especially indebted to Geraldine, who makes all things seem possible.

The ancient landmarks, one by one
    Around the old home-stead,
Are passing—going one by one
    With slow and anxious tread
And many thoughts of by gone days
    I pass from scene to scene.
At every turn some loss delays
    My steps. I pause between
The Present and the past to note
    What was, but now is not—
The pottery of days remote,
    Leaves naught to mark the spot.
But here and there a broken sherd
    And here and there a thought—
My father was a man whose word
    And deed and life were fraught
        With inspiration.

        —D. I. Suter (c. 1906)

A Potter's Progress

INTRODUCTION

Why write a book about Emanuel Suter? Or, better yet, why read a book about Emanuel Suter? There are more than a few answers to these questions, and hopefully after reading this book you will understand my reasons. Emanuel Suter was a middle-class farmer and artisan in the United States' transformative nineteenth century. He was the son of a Swiss immigrant and a second-generation American of German descent. He lived nearly his entire life in the culturally transitional region of the Shenandoah Valley in Virginia, a site that formed a migratory link between the mid-Atlantic culture of Pennsylvania and the Southern cultures south and east of the Blue Ridge Mountains. Throughout his adult life he and his family were members of the Anabaptist religious group known as Mennonites; this commitment to a community of believers who had taken advantage of America's promise of religious tolerance deeply affected Suter's decision-making in all aspects of his life. As you read further you will encounter Suter's efforts to bring his religious community out of the past toward an accepting and adaptable future. Termed "progress" by Suter, he also valued this element in his work life, earning a reputation in his community as a farmer willing to step forward to try the many innovations that American inventiveness provided in the second half of the nineteenth century. His goal was that "we realize the importance of making progress in everything we have before us, let it be secular or spiritual," and he practiced this precept diligently.[1] In one oddly postmodern moment, he wrote in his diary, "Today I purchased a phone over the phone."[2] What a marvel in 1897 for a man born in 1833. We encounter in *The Education of Henry Adams* how a New England grandson and great-grandson of United States presidents coped with this changing world; in the story of Emanuel Suter we gain a similar insight from a different socio-cultural perspective. Suter and Adams were contemporaries, Suter born in 1833 and Adams in 1838, yet they experienced the changing United States in different but equally meaningful ways. We need the stories of folks like Emanuel Suter to provide the balance necessary in accurate cultural history.

Adams told his story in a brilliant literary autobiography. Folks like Suter, however, often recorded their lives in less systematic ways, leaving behind the objects they made and used—the occasional collection of business or personal papers, ledgers, and other jottings and recollections about their lives. Telling these stories is a matter of piecing together scraps, documents, and objects that represent a portion of a life gathered by the researcher. The story told necessarily arises from the teller's interpretation of the objects and ephemera gathered. Emanuel Suter preserved his thoughts and actions over thirty-five years through a daily diary, copious quantities of personal and business correspondence, a few photographs, and, significantly, thousands of examples of utilitarian ceramic ware. While statistics of the number of pots thrown per day, month, or year could certainly tell a story of a nineteenth-century Shenandoah Valley potter's life, the biography narrated in this work concentrates on Suter's self-stated belief in progress "be it secular or spiritual." Wayne Franklin observes in his work on a nineteenth-century craftsman that "however tidy statistics are, the real lives which they manipulate resist mere summation," and this study of Emanuel Suter's ethos and production similarly does not attempt to summarize the complex life of this craftsman with numerical abstractions.[3]

Instead, examples of Suter's belief in progress in his religious, agricultural, and domestic endeavors contribute to the primary focus of this work—Suter's career as a potter and how his forward thinking represents a fundamental shift in traditional craft production in the Shenandoah Valley. The most prolific nineteenth-century traditional potter in Rockingham County, Virginia, Suter's career spanned from 1851 to 1897, a period in which he operated three pottery workshops, each moving forward technologically and culminating with a modern industrial manufactory. This study uses Suter's own words from his diaries and notebooks alongside the substantial quantity of his extant ware to explore how a chronological look at a craftsman's oeuvre, coupled with his own thoughts and the reactions of others, reveals the path of change within a traditional craft in a regional setting. In this case, Emanuel Suter supplied the documentation and the material culture evidence to evaluate the evolution of the pottery craft in the Shenandoah Valley.

Aiming their studies at the Old South, some recent historians have declared that "as a constituent element of a modernizing nation, the Old South can more easily be comprehended as oriented toward the future rather than as stuck in the past."[4] Such an outlook, I argue, can also be applied to the Shenandoah Valley, although culturally the region had little to do with what has been identified as the Old South. Nineteenth-century residents of the region were keenly aware of this distinction. Certainly slavery, an essential element of Old South culture and economy, existed in the Shenandoah Valley; however, opposition to the slave trade based on the conservative religious beliefs of many Valley landholders made the ownership of slaves less common in some communities of the region. As a follower of the Mennonite faith, Emanuel Suter and most members of his cultural community never owned slaves. Chapter One explores the nature of the Shenandoah Valley as a region and differentiates the Valley from the Old South of eastern Virginia. As this entire study endeavors to show, while the Shenandoah Valley fits the description of a South "oriented toward the future," familial connections, religion, language, and material culture illustrate clearly dominant cultural ties to the mid-Atlantic region down the valley, primarily in Pennsylvania. This chapter sets the stage for Emanuel Suter's strong connection with this region and helps explain his willingness to look even farther afield as the pottery industry moved westward.

Chapter Two offers a biography of Suter that focuses on his vision of progress and how he applied that conviction to aspects of his faith, his approach to farming, and even to his domestic space. His questioning of the Mennonite method of choosing ministers and his advocacy of Sunday Schools in the church placed him at the forefront of controversial change within the denomination. Similarly, I demonstrate that his adoption and promotion of innovative and time-saving agricultural techniques also reflect his progressive attitude. Ultimately, he brought these ideas home by completely remodeling his house according to current tastes.

Chapters Three and Four combined form the primary focus of this book. These chapters explore Suter's application of his progressive attitudes in the craft and business of pottery production. Chapter Three details Suter's work at the potteries on his New Erection, Virginia, farm from 1855 to 1890. Specifics of his connection with the Cowden and Wilcox Pottery in Harrisburg, Pennsylvania, demonstrate that decisions he made upon returning to the Shenandoah Valley in 1865 reflect a different understanding of the craft from the tradition in which he had learned. Close study of his techniques, products, materials, tools, shop organization, marketing, and labor reveal the revolutionary role that Suter's shop played in the traditional world of Rockingham County pottery manufacture. Chapter Four turns the focus to the Harrisonburg Steam Pottery Company, which was incorporated in 1890. This endeavor exemplifies the final step in Suter's move to the corporate world from the community-based craft world in which he was raised. Once this shift occurred, Suter continued to turn pots occasionally; however, his primary role was that of president of the company, a position he maintained until 1897. The focus on the technology at the pottery— including descriptions of the kiln and jigger wheels along with details about the products, materials, marketing, and labor—describes the final step in the evolution of Rockingham County pottery manufacture.

This exploration of Emanuel Suter's thoughts and attitudes relating to agriculture, religion, home life, and the pottery industry illuminate the adaptation of traditions in the Shenandoah Valley. Regionally significant traditions such as language, religion, and some architectural designs did persist after the second half of the nineteenth century; however, many aspects of traditional community life did not survive. By focusing on the life and progressive outlook of one craftsman, this study uncovers one path that led from traditional ways of organizing life in a community to a modern viewpoint in the Shenandoah Valley region. In doing so it achieves two goals: it offers an example of how a study of the life of a craftsman can elucidate larger issues in the study of American culture, and more specifically, it contributes to the history of ceramics in the United States by exploring the impetus of change from tradition to industry.

Chapter One

THE SHENANDOAH VALLEY AS A CULTURAL REGION

"that beautiful valley, the place of my birth"

Emanuel Suter, "A Letter from Harrisburg, Pa.,"
Herald of Truth 2, no. 4 (1865): 29

Events in the Civil War illustrate the geographical significance of the Shenandoah Valley to both the North and South and demonstrate the greater regional importance of the Valley area in the nineteenth century.[1] Dubbed the "bread basket of the Confederacy," the fertile agricultural lands of the Valley were the focus of numerous invasions from the Union army and provided the unique topographical features that made possible General Thomas "Stonewall" Jackson's celebrated Valley Campaign of 1862. The attention paid to this area of the commonwealth by both governments highlights its geographical importance. In 1863, Confederate General Robert E. Lee used the Valley as a springboard for his offensive thrust that culminated at Gettysburg, Pennsylvania. On the other hand, as General Philip Sheridan proved, a strong move southward through the Shenandoah Valley could have devastating results on the Southern cause—both mentally and physically. His burning raid in 1864 signaled the beginning of the end for the Confederacy.[2]

It was that incursion, however, which provided the impetus for many Valley residents to move northward to Pennsylvania as refugees. Having remained loyal to the Union throughout the conflict, it is not surprising that many residents chose to move out of the South, a move that signified their allegiance not only to the Union but to the mindset of the mid-Atlantic and northern regions of the United States. When questioned by the Southern Claims Commission in 1871, Emanuel Suter testified, "At the beginning of the war I sympathized with the Union. I voted for the ordinance of secession. It was against my conviction. I was forced to it. After its adoption I adhered to the cause of the Union and did not go with my state."[3] An opponent to the war, Suter chose to move his family out of the Valley during Sheridan's 1864 raid, traveling north and settling near Mechanicsburg, Pennsylvania.

After spending nearly six wearisome months as a refugee in Pennsylvania, Emanuel Suter wrote to the editor of the Mennonite journal *Herald of Truth*: "my mind is sometimes unconsciously carried back to those blue mountains of Virginia—to that beautiful valley, the place of my birth, where I spent my boyhood's days in innocent glee, and grew up to years of maturity; yes, all these beautiful scenes, friends, relations, brothers and sisters, have won in my heart the warmest affections, and it is hard to forget them."[4] Suter's reminiscence of the Shenandoah Valley reveals a truly ardent desire to return to the landscape of his home. Moreover, the letter's origin in south-central Pennsylvania illustrates the unique tie that many Shenandoah Valley residents had with that region. Opposed to bearing arms, many followers of the Swiss and German sects of the Mennonite and Brethren faiths fled from the Valley into Pennsylvania. Many, like Emanuel Suter and his family, followed General Sheridan out of the Valley in 1864 as refugees, working and staying with their kin and spiritual brethren in that state.[5]

Brief narratives such as these suggest that, although in the eighteenth century the Valley primarily provided a migration route *out* of Pennsylvania, by the mid-nineteenth century the flow of people, goods, and ideas was beginning to move in both directions. No longer a frontier, the Shenandoah Valley was an agricultural center producing goods that were taken on the Philadelphia Wagon Road through southeastern Pennsylvania to the port city of Philadelphia and elsewhere. As a result of trade and kinship patterns, many similarities exist between the cultural lives of the Shenandoah Valley and south-central Pennsylvania.[6]

Familial and religious connections in Pennsylvania were not simply coincidences; for more than a century the main road through the Shenandoah Valley had served as a major migration route for immigrants and migrants heading south from Pennsylvania.[7] This migration route—variously known as the Philadelphia Wagon Road, the Great Valley Road, and later US Route 11 and Interstate 81—carried not only people but also their knowledge, ideas, and cultural heritage. Many of these traits are still evident in the Valley of Virginia and certainly were so in the nineteenth century when Emanuel Suter married, raised a family, and operated a successful farm and business in the Shenandoah Valley. These cultural links, along with the trade and industrial opportunities that lay down the valley, made Pennsylvania an important place for residents of the Shenandoah Valley in the nineteenth century—not the least for the potter Emanuel Suter.[8]

By examining the interaction between environment (site) and the cultural traditions (situation) of a region, geographers interpret the unique dynamics of that area; such an approach may be applied to the Shenandoah Valley.[9] Since this study is cultural rather than geologic, it is prudent at this point to merely note that an abundance of potters in the Shenandoah Valley in the nineteenth century attests to the source of good clay within the region.[10] Suter was able to dig clay for earthenware on his own and surrounding farms and usually travelled less than twenty-five miles for stoneware clay. The Valley was, then, a good site for potters.

But what of the situation of the Valley—its spatial relation to other cultural developments? Geographically, the Shenandoah Valley is part of a unique natural valley that provides a physical link between the northern and southern United States. The Shenandoah Valley stretches 180 miles southwestward from the Potomac River at Harpers Ferry, West Virginia, to just south of Lexington, Virginia.[11] The valley itself is bordered by the Blue Ridge to the east and the first ridges of the Alleghenies to the west. Beginning near Strasburg and running in a south-westerly direction approximately fifty-five miles, the Massanutten Mountain bisects the central valley and separates the north and south forks of the Shenandoah River. This stretch of the Great Valley between Harpers Ferry and Lexington affords the largest and most fertile agricultural area in the Virginia Appalachians, offering immigrants and migrants a natural travel route as well as a good reason to linger in the region.[12]

Initial European occupancy and migration through the Valley follows the history of westward expansion in the United States—including the difficulty of finding affordable land in Pennsylvania and the relationship between the British, and later American, government and the French and Indians.

Although the Valley was known to trappers and traders in the seventeenth century, the first permanent settlements of European immigrants there did not arise until the 1720s. By that time European expansion from Virginia's Tidewater had forced rival Indian tribes from the Piedmont westward into the Valley where they used the natural route to travel north and south for trading and wars. Along with intermittent contact with Indians, speculating British landlords were encouraging settlement in the Valley to provide a buffer zone between the volatile tribes in the west and the constantly unstable situation created by the French west of the Alleghenies.[13] While many pioneers in the late eighteenth century passed through the Valley on their way to Tennessee, the Carolinas, Kentucky, and beyond, large numbers of German-speaking peoples settled in the Shenandoah Valley, farming the rich land and forming communities.[14] With families and friends in Pennsylvania, these settlers naturally looked northward to the mid-Atlantic as their cultural hearth, not to the South.

Obviously, this link existed well before the division of the nation during the Civil War and before Emanuel Suter and others used the route to escape the destruction of the region in 1864. Residents of the Valley maintained economic ties to Pennsylvania as early as the mid-eighteenth century,[15] and, although trade routes were also opened over the Blue Ridge Mountains to the east, by the turn of the nineteenth century, as Robert Mitchell notes, the "backbone of this network was the Great Wagon Road along which the region's major settlements were located and from which branched a small number of east-west secondary roads linking the valley with eastern Virginia at Winchester and Staunton."[16]

These trade routes induced both change and continuity in the Shenandoah Valley. While initial immigrants to the region settled in ethnic pockets and constructed their environment according to traditional methods, as the century progressed these groups became more involved with the economy of the region as a whole and began to integrate their lives with other residents of the Valley. Several factors contributed to this assimilation, including the construction of new and better transportation routes and the growth of nationalistic sentiments following the American Revolutionary War. Although Mitchell suggests that the "varied expressions of pluralism and regionalism that were so characteristic of the colonial period of the eighteenth century were hybridized and reduced,"[17] material evidence still conspicuous on the landscape and in the objects created during the nineteenth century suggests that cultural and ethnic ties *were* preserved whenever possible.

Although the Shenandoah Valley was settled by groups with several ethnic backgrounds—most notably Germans, Swiss, English, and Scots-Irish—I deal solely with elements of German and Swiss culture evident in the Shenandoah Valley. Such a concentration is appropriate for several reasons. The focus of this study—Emanuel Suter and his times—is set within a specific location with specific characteristics. Suter lived his entire life in Rockingham County, a county with a large population with German and Swiss ancestry; his own family was of Swiss and German background.[18] A majority of this group in the county, including Suter, followed the religious denominations of the Mennonite church and the Church of the Brethren, or German Baptists (Dunkards) as they were known in the nineteenth century. A tour through the Shenandoah Valley quickly attests to the influence of Germanic and Swiss cultures; it is nearly impossible to drive for more than a mile through the countryside without spying a large forebay barn—a clear symbol of early and lasting influences on the region.[19]

A survey of cultural features such as language, religion, and architecture shows that ties to Pennsylvania remain evident in the twenty-first-century Shenandoah Valley, suggesting that in the nineteenth century such links were even stronger. For instance, when Suter and his fellow refugees fled north in 1864, they would have felt comfort knowing that they would be amongst people who literally "spoke the same language." Similarly, a nineteenth-century traveler heading south from Pennsylvania might find that the dialect he heard was not significantly different until he reached the area just south of the James River. The early German settlements in the Valley used their native language to communicate, easily forming a link with their neighbors to the north, and as the nineteenth century approached, this did not change completely.[20] Although the various ethnic cultures of the region did begin to assimilate and communicate with the broader area of the East Coast of the United States, these groups—particularly those from German-speaking lands—continued to speak a form of their own language amongst themselves.[21] A form of German language known as "Dutch" can still be heard in the Shenandoah Valley today, although it is not nearly as common as it once was. Many Rockingham County residents of German and Swiss descent recall the dialect being spoken by their parents, and in the early twenty-first century the language continues to be spoken in some homes.[22]

Linguists have shown this pattern to coincide with other links between the Shenandoah Valley and the Pennsylvania culture region. Paralleling the regions Henry Glassie identified in his study of the material culture of the eastern United States, Hans Kurath's word geography of the same area finds many of the same results.[23] Dividing the eastern portion of the country into three sections—North, Midland, and South—Kurath identifies the southern boundary of the Midland region as the "crest of the Blue Ridge in Virginia." Dividing the region further, he suggests that the Shenandoah Valley should be included in the section consisting of eastern Pennsylvania and western New Jersey. Kurath comments that in some usage, such as cattle calls, the "Pennsylvania Germans have largely retained their German calls in Eastern Pennsylvania, the Shenandoah Valley, and northern West Virginia,"[24] adding that "some expressions of Pennsylvania German origin are current not only in the eastern part of the state but also in sections where Pennsylvania German is now little used or extinct, as in . . . the Shenandoah Valley."[25] Naturally, at the time of settlement in the eighteenth century, German was a common language in the Shenandoah Valley.[26]

Only the religious ties to a Germanic culture overshadow the importance of language to the Pennsylvanian German cultural group of the Shenandoah Valley. A story that has been recorded many times, immigration of large numbers of Mennonites and Brethren from the Netherlands and the Palatinate region of Germany to the American colonies in the eighteenth century added to the mid-Atlantic population.[27] In this context, however, it must be emphasized that these groups settled originally in the colony of Pennsylvania beginning in 1683 and that by the mid-eighteenth century families of Germans and Pennsylvanians of German ancestry began to move into the Shenandoah Valley.[28] As early as 1776, groups of German Baptists and Mennonites began to move into the Valley, reacting to, as Klaus Wust points out, "events of the war, outright persecution in some cases, and the pressure of their ever increasing families."[29] By 1908, Rockingham County had the largest membership in the German Baptist church in the state, followed closely by Augusta County.[30] Similarly, a map of German congregations in 1810 shows a large number of Mennonite communities in Rockingham County. The county remains the center of Mennonite culture in Virginia, testifying to the maintenance of cultural heritage among those of German and Swiss ancestry.[31]

Warren Hofstra and Karl Raitz emphasize that "landscape elements provide one of the most useful tools in the geographer's workshop for constructing regions and understanding regional identity."[32] As their assertion indicates, while speech and religion are important indicators of cultural heritage in the Shenandoah Valley, the ubiquity of the Pennsylvania barn on the landscape presents a striking visual testimony to the influence of Swiss and German culture on the region. While other material features of culture also reveal close ties, none are as noticeable as the substantial barn with its projecting forebay and sloping barn bridge. Stressing the Valley Road's significance to cultural transference, Hofstra and Raitz maintain that it "was down the road that Pennsylvania migrants carried the idea of the Pennsylvania barn from its American cultural hearth."[33]

Many barns and houses were destroyed by the Union forces, and a massive and literal reconstruction took place following Lee's surrender in April of 1865. The rebuilding of structures burned during Sheridan's 1864 raid on the Valley indicates the cultural significance of the barn-building tradition. The rebuilt barns were not constructed according to new and different designs; rather, Valley farmers built with the old, time-tested plan of a two-level barn with a cantilevered forebay. In such a climate, skilled craftsmen were necessary, especially those with the knowledge of how the structure should be built. Writing to his father who had spent the final war years with relatives in the Midwest, Emanuel Suter commented that "the people think you ought to come home to help to build barns. . . . There is no doubt but what you could do well here now. The people are making preparations for rebuilding their Barns again."[34] Such remarks clearly illustrate the need for one who possessed an understanding of barn construction and consequently suggest that the traditional way was still the best way. Regarding this adherence to a particular type, Joseph Glass points out that they are "testimony to a common agreement by masses of farmers about the appropriateness of their physical appearance and about the functional utility of that physical form. Collectively, they serve as a surrogate measure of the extent of the area through which these and other shared ideas, thought processes, and farming activities prevailed."[35] Taken together these examples illustrate the relationship between place and ideas and illuminate the importance of the geographical "situation" of the Valley to the ideas that helped shape Emanuel Suter's life and pottery career.

Ultimately for Suter, the geographical situation of the Shenandoah Valley encouraged both a traditional way of life and a progressive move towards the industrialization characteristic of the nation in the last quarter of the nineteenth century. With Pennsylvania culture a part of his heritage and his surroundings, Suter traveled down the Shenandoah Valley into that mid-Atlantic state, taking advantage of the opportunities offered by such a trip. Prior to his 1865 stint at the Cowden and Wilcox pottery in Harrisburg, Suter had never seen a "large" pottery in operation. After this revelation of just how his more traditional business might someday work, he expanded the size of his shop and kiln and increasingly sought new ways of producing ware. Using his experience in Pennsylvania as a springboard, he eventually extended his horizons to New York, New Jersey, Ohio, and West Virginia, calling on family connections as well as those from the business world.

This reasoning may appear contradictory: if Suter lived within a region of highly identifiable traits, his movement toward change in that region suggests that the region was not stable but was, instead, variable and perhaps not a region at all. On the contrary, the Shenandoah Valley did maintain the ethnic characteristics addressed above; however, these features form the basis for a study of change *within* the region. Cultural geographers Wilbur Zelinsky and Michael Conzen suggest that regional study is a viable way to understand "community" despite the changes that occur within traditional regions. Zelinsky notes that, in spite of the diluting effect of modernization and cultural exchange, many older cultural areas still exist. Formed by individuals who sought out "places with perceived economic advantages and/or those that kinfolk, friends, and coreligionists had previously settled in," these regions continue to reflect the cultural heritage of the nineteenth century.[36] Conzen, too, demonstrates that certain ethnic regions continue to maintain distinctive identities, citing as an example Mennonite and Amish communities in Pennsylvania and, by extension, the Shenandoah Valley.[37]

While these scholars support the validity of regional studies, Emanuel Suter's actions within a cultural region demonstrate a move toward change, not maintenance of tradition. Suter's endeavors, however, do not present a contradiction of ideas but rather demonstrate the creation of a different kind of region—a type that D. W. Meinig refers to as an industrial region.

Looked at in this light, we see that the Shenandoah Valley, while maintaining certain aspects of its ethnic heritage (language, architecture, craft traditions), changed in the nineteenth century, shifting from a region of insular communities to one inspired by regional concepts of industrialism. Emanuel Suter's progressive beliefs and actions demonstrate how some communities in the Shenandoah Valley attempted to modify their culture.

In his work Meinig demonstrates that the South, unable to support itself in industrial needs, relied heavily on the North and Europe for both materials and knowledge of industrial methods.[38] The Shenandoah Valley, however, demonstrated more affinities with Pennsylvania than with the regions to the south, and therefore its views in terms of industrialization were similarly affected by that region. Philadelphia was already a major port and manufacturing center by the mid-eighteenth century, and the city influenced Shenandoah Valley culture. That Emanuel Suter and others maintained connections in that direction demonstrates their willingness to accept a northern way of thinking.[39]

Meinig argues that industrial centers such as Philadelphia became specialized versions of cultural hearths and that their influence "spread as an increasingly integrated system to advantageous areas farther afield."[40] As cultural traits filtered into the Shenandoah Valley from Pennsylvania in the eighteenth and early nineteenth centuries, an understanding of the importance of technology and industrialization would have also been considered—if not accepted—in the Valley and beyond. Naturally, not every community along the path of cultural migration would be willing to accept all of the available concepts. Meinig points out that it is important to look at the "cultural character" of not only the hearths but to also take into consideration the "long nurture of entrepreneurial and artisanal talents that would be poised to respond to new technological and economic opportunities."[41]

John Majewski has demonstrated that, prior to the Civil War, Virginia's highly localized transportation networks limited market expansion and exposure to other regions' influences. Furthermore, he argues that "a slave society, no matter how much wealth it produced, could not compete against a northern economy that harnessed the power of ordinary households left free to invent, to improve, to invest, and to consume."[42] As essayists in *The Great Valley Road of Virginia* make plain, however, the Shenandoah Valley benefitted from its connection via the Road to northern ideas before the war, and although slavery did play a significant role in the region, it did not, as Majewski asserts, limit the creative and economic power of ordinary households, especially in the Anabaptist community in which Emanuel Suter lived and worked. As demonstrated, nineteenth-century Shenandoah Valley residents identified themselves differently from those east of the Blue Ridge Mountains. The plantation system in eastern Virginia of which Majewski writes did not dominate the Valley, and for many the "Old Virginia" cultural patterns were more foreign than the northern ordinary household culture.[43]

This study of the potter Emanuel Suter illustrates how certain individuals in the Valley responded to the ideas that traveled from these "cultural hearths." Suter, and others like him, explored new methods of production and expanded the horizons of the largely traditional communities in the Valley. Subsequent chapters will demonstrate Suter's willingness to try new methods and to explore nontraditional options in an effort to emulate his neighbors— and cultural antecedents—to the north. In so doing, progressive thinkers like Suter began to break down the traditional ties of community and ethnic identity, replacing them with regional connections based on economics and business. While the endeavor did have a lasting effect on the Shenandoah Valley, the industrial might of the hearth region never materialized in the Valley, which continues to maintain its agricultural identity.

A fervently traditional man, Suter ardently maintained his belief in the religion of his forefathers, constructed his environment in age-old ways, and learned the pottery trade from a family member; he understood where the roots of his culture lay—not to the east or south, but to the north. His location in the Shenandoah Valley afforded him a strong identification with place, and that situation helped to determine not only the methods of his craft but also how they might change. Ensuing chapters demonstrate that Suter regarded progress and innovation as seriously as he did his cultural heritage and that he understood where to look for advice on how those changes could transform his life. He looked to the north (and eventually the west) simply because generations of his family and neighbors had consistently looked there. It was tradition. It was that tradition of looking north that had a profound impact on the life and work of this potter.

Chapter Two

EMANUEL SUTER'S VISION OF PROGRESS

"May we realize the importance of making progress in everything
we have before us, let it be secular or spiritual."

Emanuel Suter Diary, 1 January 1893

The story of Emanuel Suter does not begin in the Shenandoah Valley,
but in what is now the Swiss canton of Aargau. Like their neighbors,
the Suters were tenant farmers for wealthy landowners near the village of
Kölliken, in addition to being skillful shoemakers, tanners, cabinetmakers,
and weavers. Before the turn of the nineteenth century, Emanuel Suter's
great-grandfather fled from Switzerland with his family across the French
border into the southern Alsace region in response to their persecution as
Anabaptists. The Suters settled in Lepuix, France, where they continued as
highly valued tenant cattle farmers. Daniel Suter, Emanuel Suter's father,
was born there on October 5, 1806.[1] From there Daniel, along with several
of his siblings, began his journey to the United States in the mid-1820s.

In 1824, Daniel's brother Christian immigrated to the United States,
and by 1826 other family members had journeyed to America. Daniel joined
his brother in Rockingham County, Virginia, and worked as a cabinetmaker
and carpenter. Within two years, he married Anna Heatwole (Hütwhol),
settling near Dayton, Virginia. Anna was a daughter of David and Magdalene
Heatwole; her family had moved to the Shenandoah Valley in 1797, leaving
Franklin County, Pennsylvania, in the region where David's father had settled

after arriving from Steeg bei Bacharach in the Rhine Valley of Germany.[2] Before her death in 1835, Anna Heatwole Suter gave birth to five children. Born on March 26, 1833, Emanuel Suter was the fourth child of the marriage. Following custom, upon his mother's death, Emanuel and his brothers and sisters moved into the homes of various relatives.

From the age of two, Emanuel lived with the family of his uncle and aunt Samuel (Shem) Heatwole and Elizabeth Shank Heatwole, growing up on a farm on Linville Creek, north of the town of Harrisonburg. Little is known of his life there, although Suter's 1896 mention in his diary of visiting the area reveals that he held pleasant memories of the time he spent there. He wrote: "This afternoon I walked around over the ground that I used to run over when I was a small school boy. I located the place where the school house used to stand [and] I visited a cave in close proximity us boys use [*sic*] to enter. I also visited flowing and ebbing spring on above named place us school boys used to visit. This remarkable spring, its waters are as clear as cristle [*sic*] as it flows away. It runs about 10 minutes at a time strong enough to turn a mill."[3] The farm on which the family lived was the home of Elizabeth's parents; Shem Heatwole eventually moved his family back to his ancestral home near Dayton, Virginia, until the death of his father in 1842. Shortly afterwards, Heatwole traded farms with Jonathan Clary and relocated to property at the confluence of Beaver and Spring creeks in the southwest corner of Rockingham County.[4] Along with farming, Heatwole also operated a saw mill. Considered one of the family, Emanuel Suter moved along with the Heatwoles, spending his life from the age of ten to eighteen in the village of Spring Creek. In 1855, Emanuel Suter married Elizabeth Swope, and the two moved west of Harrisonburg to the farm of her father, Reuben Swope. The couple remained there the rest of their lives. Emanuel died on December 16, 1902, and Elizabeth died on October 10, 1923.

• • •

When he faced the attorney for the Southern Claims Commission in 1871, Emanuel Suter responded to the opening question by stating, "I am a farmer. I have lived where I now do since 1855, except from Oct. 5, 1864 to June 1865 when I went to Penn. I worked in Harrisburg at my trade. I returned home in June 1865."[5] These facts are certain, but Suter's distinction between farming and his trade is perhaps most significant: he clearly differentiated the work of farming and producing pottery. In 1851, at the age of eighteen and uncertain about his future as a farmer, Suter most likely found the craft of pottery a well-respected and desirable trade during a time that demanded the products of skilled potters. In his "Sketch of the Life and Work of Emanuel Suter" for the *Mennonite Year-Book and Directory*, L. J. Heatwole notes that at the age of eighteen Suter went to live in the Dry River neighborhood with his cousin John D. Heatwole, from whom he learned the potter's trade.[6] Heatwole was Suter's first cousin and his elder by nearly five years. While no formal papers are extant to reveal an apprentice-type relationship between John D. Heatwole and Emanuel Suter, many of Suter's early pottery forms as well as oral history testify to the master–student relationship between the two.

Suter also surely learned much from Heatwole's father-in-law and teacher, Andrew Coffman. Born in New Market, Virginia, in 1795 and trained by the Hagerstown-born potters Jacob and Christian Adam, Coffman has been credited with introducing what has come to be known as the Rockingham County style of pottery.[7] The material evidence of Suter's pottery clearly illustrates a connection to both of these potters. The arrangements between Suter, Heatwole, and Coffman remain unknown, but the earliest dated piece of Suter's ware, dated "1851" and signed "Emanuel" in cobalt, shows a clear influence by both potters (fig. 1). Most likely Suter worked with Heatwole from 1851 throughout the decade. Heatwole had formed a "company" by 1853, stenciling some ware with the label "J. D. Heatwole/ & Co. Potters/ Rockingham/ Va."; Suter, along with Reuben Coffman (a son of Andrew), produced ware for Heatwole during this period.[8] Documentary evidence also places Suter with Heatwole in the early 1850s. Suter's tax receipt for 1854 notes that he was living on Heatwole's "tract," and both Suter and Heatwole signed a "note" dated September 20, 1854, binding themselves to pay John Funkhouser.[9]

The life of a craftsman was a logical choice for Suter who grew up in a period when hand-crafted objects were standard. Shem Heatwole was a carpenter as well as a farmer, and, although Emanuel Suter did not have the benefit of his father's tutelage, the elder Suter was a respected cabinetmaker. One of Suter's older brothers, David, was also a craftsman, earning a living throughout his life as a wheelwright and wagon maker.[10] Although primarily a potter, Emanuel Suter also occasionally built furniture, and at least one of his own sons was a cabinetmaker.[11]

On August 26, 1855, Emanuel Suter married Elizabeth Swope, and the couple settled on her father's farm, located approximately four miles west of Harrisonburg, Virginia, in the community known as New Erection (fig. 2).[12] The land was subsequently deeded to Suter by his father-in-law, Reuben Swope, in January of 1859, and this farm of eventually 140 acres became the site of Suter's farming and initial pottery operations. Little is known regarding Suter between the years 1851 and 1855. However, several signed and dated pots indicate that he was making pottery in 1851; numerous pots, including a double-handled stoneware jug with the inscription "August the 5 1864," demonstrate that he was making pottery prior to leaving the Valley in that year.[13] Testimony from one of Suter's witnesses in the Southern Claims Commission case corroborates the existence of Suter's earliest pottery enterprise. Responding to the question of what Emanuel Suter was doing during the war, David A. Heatwole recalled, "I think he was farming and was making and was running a potter's kill [kiln] part of the time." He added that Suter sold his ware "around among the country people," and that he did not sell it to the Confederate Quartermaster or any agents of the Confederacy.[14] A note from May 11, 1864, records that Suter sold George Gowl a one-and-a-half-gallon pot—five months before leaving the Shenandoah Valley for Pennsylvania.[15]

Prior to the Civil War, on November 1, 1857, the Suters joined the Mennonite Church, a connection that would have a profound influence on Emanuel Suter.[16] Pacifists by doctrine, Mennonites opposed the Civil War and refused to fight, leading many young men to evade conscription by fleeing northward during the conflict or hiding within the community.[17] The Suter family eventually joined the exodus, and Emanuel's subsequent employment by the Cowden and Wilcox pottery in Harrisburg, Pennsylvania, introduced the young man to innovative ideas and designs.[18] When he returned to Virginia in 1865, he immediately set about turning ware again, and by August of 1866, he reported in his diary that "This forenoon father and myself were makeing out a draft of my potter shop."[19] A month later he noted: "This forenoon we laid off my potter kiln. Samuel Shrum & hands commenced working on the kiln."[20]

What led Suter to feel the need for a new shop and kiln, and on what basis did he design these structures? Clearly his experience in Pennsylvania stimulated his imagination and broadened his business sense, but choices that he made evince that he was also willing to question and change other facets of his life. His response to his religion and his farming techniques suggest that Suter realized the value of progress and recognized its necessity. An advocate for change, Suter sought to adjust aspects of his life in order to increase efficiency, often considering the common good.[21]

EMANUEL SUTER AND THE MENNONITE CHURCH

"Hold fast to the bible as the Sure anchor of our liberties.
Write its precepts on your hearts and practice them in your lives.
To the influence of this book we are indebted for the progress made in true civilization and to this we must look as our guide in the future."

—Emanuel Suter Diary, Memoranda Page, 1886

Perhaps Suter's adherence to the doctrine of the Mennonite Church sparked his interest in progress. Common misconceptions of the conservatism of the Mennonites may make this seem unlikely; however, the Mennonite Church has always had its progressive factions, and many view this as a characteristic of the church. Theron F. Schlabach, a scholar of nineteenth-century Mennonite culture, asserts that, for the Mennonite, "Progressivism was faith that change—new institutions, new practices—usually meant improvement, not a falling away. It was faith in 'progress.'"[22] This study illustrates that such "faith" can be traced throughout Suter's life, not only in his relations with the church but in his businesses as well.

To explain the origins, beliefs, and various denominations of the Mennonite Church in America is beyond the scope of this work; however, several examples of disagreement within the church illustrate important discussions in the nineteenth-century group. Conflicts over the method of choosing ministers and the value of holding Sunday schools, for example, led to controversy in various communities, and in Virginia eventually resulted in a schism within the church. Emanuel Suter's stances on these matters exemplify his belief in progress as it applied to religious matters.

Suter was a Christian and lived his life with Christian precepts in mind.[23] Within a few years of his baptism into the church, the Civil War began; as a member of a pacifist denomination, he felt strongly against serving in the Confederate armed forces and legally furnished a substitute, later relieving that man by paying a $500 exemption fine.[24] Like many of his fellow church members, he was also opposed to Virginia's secession from the Union, a belief that placed him in opposition to many of his non-Anabaptist neighbors in Rockingham County. Demonstrating his standing in the Mennonite community, when a group of young church members were imprisoned in Libby Prison in Richmond for refusing to serve, Suter was sent with church-raised funds to secure the release of his fellow church members.[25]

Following the Civil War, Suter continued to play an active role in the Mennonite community. Like other members, he participated in building new churches in the area and contributed to several significant church committees. From the late 1870s to 1890, Suter served on a committee to revise, and eventually compile, a new hymnbook for the Mennonite Church.[26] He also served as the secretary for the Virginia Mennonite Conference from October 1886 through October of 1894, further demonstrating the confidence that church members had in his leadership.[27] Suter's obituary in the *Herald of Truth* attests to his high standing in the community. Bishop L. J. Heatwole noted that: "Suter was perhaps the most widely known and beloved of any one in the community in which he lived, and it would seem impossible to find his counterpart, or have the vacancy in the community that has been caused by his death, to be filled by anyone else as he filled it."[28] Despite this high praise and obvious respect, Emanuel Suter did question certain tenets of the Mennonite doctrine, making his opposition to those rules known to other members of the church.

One of those was the Mennonite Church's strict doctrine for choosing ministers. In the nineteenth century, Mennonites chose the men who would minister to their congregations by drawing lots, a process that included the congregation first voting for candidates. Once candidates were selected, the bishop would place a collection of hymnbooks or Bibles equal to the number of candidates on a table in front of the congregation. One volume would hold a slip of paper with the quotation from the book of Proverbs: "The lot is cast into the lap; but the whole disposing thereof is of the Lord." Each candidate would select a book from the table, and the one who found the slip was believed to have been chosen by God to serve as a minister.[29] That Suter disagreed with this procedure must have been no surprise to many church members. On several occasions he was voted into candidacy, but he never succeeded in choosing the book with the scripture in it. This was particularly distressing for Suter, for he sincerely felt that he was "called" to the ministry.

Two letters to him indicate that he was seeking advice on the matter from his church brethren. In March of 1879, Bishop Jacob Hildebrand wrote: "And as regards your conviction as to the ministry I have no doubt in my mind as to your honesty and Dear Brother if I had the control over the matter it would soon be decided. But that is the great trouble[.] Church traditions without scripture has often caused divisions and trouble."[30] Suter was either seeking advice on how to go forward or support for backing a petition to the Virginia Mennonite Conference asking to change the method of selecting ministers. Hildebrand, understanding the trouble that might arise from such a venture, only sympathized with his friend, and "Church traditions" suggests that he was reminding Suter of the importance of adhering to doctrines that had their basis in scripture.

Suter was not convinced that his cause was lost for in March of the following year he received another letter responding to what must have been a similar plea. Written by Lewis J. Heatwole, a young almanac maker who would eventually be ordained a bishop in the Mennonite Church, the letter reveals Suter's argument for suspending the use of the lot in choosing ministers: "If I comprehend your meaning, the "unalterable rule" you make mention of, is the Lot itself, and in connection you do not hesitate to say that the Church, by holding exclusively to this method of choosing her ministers, has committed an error, and sustain the assertion by stating the historic fact that the Church in her primitive days, had no occasion, nor did she seek to choose her ministers by that method."[31] Heatwole, like Hildebrand, supports the Church position; however, he also notes that, "I for one feel safe to say that the Church as a body, does not harbor any ill will toward you for taking exception to a rule which in your mind is such a barrier between yourself and the gospel ministry."[32] Heatwole's comments indicate that Suter's feelings toward the lot were well known in the congregation and that, as is stated, he was not shunned for his thoughts. Ultimately, we must see Suter's idea as part of the "progressivism" of the church. Although the issue was finally brought before the Virginia Mennonite Conference in 1894 when an amendment failed to pass, the process for choosing ministers was eventually changed, and today few churches continue the use of the lot in the ordination process.[33]

Suter also supported Sunday schools in the Mennonite Church. Although the schools had been allowed in the Virginia churches as early as 1867, there was much debate among church members regarding their usefulness and scriptural validity.[34] Many objected on the grounds that the movement had originated in popular churches and that such schools, being taught by laymen, would draw members away from the biblical understandings of the Mennonite faith. On the other hand, supporters felt that Sunday schools would provide a vehicle to teach the traditional Mennonite principles of separatism, nonconformity, and nonresistance.[35]

From the beginning of the controversy, Suter was a partisan for the schools. In 1871 and 1872, when the schools were in the initial stages of organization, he was a prime organizer for the Middle District in Virginia.[36] Despite his, and others', ardent work, the Sunday schools in Virginia were closed for nearly ten years; however, in 1881 Suter helped organize a Sunday school at Pine Grove school, a structure near a local Mennonite church. Ultimately, he was chosen superintendent of the school; although this school was not affiliated with the Mennonite Church, early leaders were Mennonites, and many young Mennonite men and women attended the exercises. Finally, in April of 1882, with the hope of keeping a tighter control over the subjects and intentions of the schools, two Sunday schools were opened in area Mennonite churches.[37]

The question finally came before the Virginia Mennonite Conference in 1894. Throughout the many years of controversy, Suter never wavered in his goal of opening and legitimizing the schools. His leadership in the movement was recognized outside of the Shenandoah Valley; in 1896 he was asked to speak on the subject of "Qualifications of a Sunday School Superintendent" at a Sunday school conference held in Scottdale, Pennsylvania.[38] In describing Suter's contributions to the movement, Mennonite historian Harry Brunk declares: "Suter's approach was not by words but by action; he was the organizer of Sunday school par excellence."[39] Brunk's assessment summarizes Suter's religious life well.

THE MODERN FARMER

"The farmer of to-day is not the dull plodder of the past."

Augustin Taveau, Report of the Commissioner
of Agriculture for 1874, 280

During this time period, Suter's mind was not entirely occupied by church issues; naturally, he was also concerned with the maintenance of his farm and business, and the progressiveness reflected in his spiritual thoughts is equally apparent in his agricultural methods. In fact, he stands out as an example of the "modern farmer" described by Augustin L. Taveau in 1875: "The farmer of to-day is not the dull plodder of the past; if he would occupy the front rank, he is called upon to use his brains as well as his hands. And he who now sows according to the changes of the moon, or sows, tills, and reaps with awkward old-fashioned tools, will be out-stripped in the race with the farmer of progress; who, while working with his brains, throws the burden of muscular labor upon the powerful sinews of his team or steam."[40]

Unlike much of the Deep South, where local economies and unfavorable growing conditions hampered farmers, the climate and soil of the Shenandoah Valley were favorable for food crops, and thus farmers in the Valley were not tied to the southern cash crops of cotton and tobacco.[41] Like his family ties and religion, Suter's crops and farming techniques connected him with the agricultural life of Pennsylvania and, as the nineteenth century progressed, to the Midwest.

Many craftsmen were also landowners and farmers, and Suter's early life would have included acquiring the knowledge and skills required for successful farming in the Shenandoah Valley. Valley farmers of the 1850s exhibited several general characteristics that offer insight into the proficiencies that Emanuel Suter would have attained as he matured on a Rockingham County farm. Typical Shenandoah Valley farmers produced food for themselves and their families and raised wheat or corn as cash crops to be sold for profit in the markets. Kenneth Koons demonstrates that during "the late antebellum period, a large majority of Valley farmers cultivated wheat—96 percent in 1850 and 90 percent in 1860." Here Koons identifies a crop that Suter needed to master as a young Valley farmer at mid-century.[42] Koons also notes that this concentration on wheat existed "within a system of mixed agriculture, the central feature of which was diversity of enterprise."[43] Spending his early years on large farms, Suter would have participated in this agricultural world and carried that knowledge with him as he established his own farm in 1855. In fact, Suter's diary includes details of the work required to manage a diverse farming operation in addition to his year-round pottery manufacturing. Suter's 140-acre farm included wheat fields, orchards, timothy grass, clover, flax, and a variety of livestock including cattle, pigs, and sheep. His apple orchard produced not only fruit for the family but served as another cash crop. Growing more than thirty varieties of apples on the seven-and-a-half-acre orchard, he dealt with numerous commission merchants in cities such as Baltimore and Washington, DC.[44] Suter's petition to the Southern Claims Commission also sheds light on the diversity of his farm. He claimed that on or around October 2, 1864, the following items and stock were taken by the United States Army:

> 20 bushels of wheat
> 5 cattle
> 10 sheep
> 1800 pounds of pork
> 2 colts
> 4 sets housing
> 15 bushels of oats

This list contributes to the portrait of a farmer established for nearly ten years and serves as a neat representation of the agricultural diversity described by Koons. Suter represents the typical nineteenth-century Shenandoah Valley farmer; however, he moved beyond the traditional farming model of his region and adopted innovations or, as he called them, "progressive" ideas relative to his farm and business.

Following the Civil War, several factors combined to increase agricultural production in the northern states. A reaction to the labor shortage caused by the war led to a move from manpower to horsepower while the opening of the West to farming increased the need for more economical and efficient ways of working the land; these changes in turn led to innovations in the use of machinery.[45] As a large wheat-producing region, the Shenandoah Valley acted more like these northern states than its neighbors to the south. Much of the land in the Valley was planted in wheat, and many of the new ideas and techniques were adopted there. Emanuel Suter's approval and advocacy of increasingly available technology further illustrate his tendency toward progressive thought.[46]

Threshing the grain of a large wheat crop consumed much time and effort. Prior to the mid-nineteenth century, this entailed a group of men pounding the cut wheat with flails, which were wooden rods with a smaller rod attached to the end by rope or leather allowing it to swing freely.[47] As early as the 1830s, the development of the threshing machine expanded rapidly, but it was not until a decade later that an efficient and inexpensive machine encouraged most farmers to switch from flailing to mechanical threshing. By 1860, advanced machines that could winnow, sort, and even bag the grain were in use in the larger wheat-producing areas of the country; however, most farmers who possessed one most likely owned a simple thresher that separated the grain from the straw.[48]

As was the case with Emanuel Suter, often one farmer in an area would purchase a more advanced machine and do custom work for his neighbors. Suter, together with his younger half-brother Jacob, purchased a threshing machine, and they put it to work throughout their community. Although the date of its purchase is unknown, Suter first mentions the machine in July of 1872: "I went to T. Atchison to see him about getting his crop to thrash, then on my way home I stopped at D. Hartman's on the same business."[49] Later that month he notes that: "To day we were threshing, quit this evening at supper then the Machine went down to John Coffman's."[50] Although the Suters purchased the thresher between the fall of 1871 and summer of 1872, Suter had worked with threshing machines as early as the first summer after his return from Pennsylvania.[51]

The Suter brothers seem to have continued to thresh for their neighbors over the next several years and, although there is no mention in Emanuel Suter's diaries of selling the thresher, they appear to have discontinued such custom work as early as 1875. Suter was a tinkerer with machinery, but perhaps the expense, frustration, and time consumed in maintaining a threshing machine led him to eventually grow weary of the business. His accounts show that the total expenses paid out for the machine in 1872 equaled $85.27 1/2, a figure that reflects many repairs. Suter also appears to have attempted to work on the machine himself. A letter from Garver and Flanagan, the Hagerstown, Maryland, manufacturers, indicates that his work was not always to his advantage: "we are not surprised to hear that the machine performed badly as the substitute of the belt in place of rakes would make it work to a great disadvantage and sure to waste grain." After making several recommendations, Garver and Flanagan advised that Suter ship the machine to them and have it put in good working order at an estimated cost of fifty-two dollars.[52] Despite these costs, Suter remained in the threshing arrangement with his brother for a few more years, continually working to keep the machine functioning. In mid-July of 1875, he notes that he and Jacob "worked at our machine until night," a task they continued throughout the week until July 14, when Suter notes that, "To day Mr. Flanagan was here, the Hagerstown Machine man."[53] Flanagan must have solved the problem, for on the next day Suter writes that "Joseph Gaines & myself moved the machine down to Peter Hartman's to thrash for him tomorrow"[54] and, on the sixteenth of July, "then we moved over to Simon Burkholder's, set the machine ready to thrash for him tomorrow."[55] No records indicate when Suter finally relinquished his role in the arrangement with his brother or whether the inconvenience and cost of maintaining the threshing machine may have ultimately caused more annoyance than Suter felt it was worth. Although he may have given up the management of a threshing machine, he did not relinquish his recognition of the value of such machinery. In 1878, he wrote to a cousin in Ohio: "Farmers are now threshing out their wheat which is now mostly done with steam power which is much easier and quicker than with horse power."[56] The important fact is that he did adopt the use of what he perceived was an economically beneficial machine—a machine that was maintained by skills derived down the Valley in Maryland.

The decade following his 1865 return from Pennsylvania was one of agricultural experimentation for Emanuel Suter. Not only did he test the value of threshing for his neighbors, he also bought a reaper, another implement that, like the threshing machine, indicates a move from hand to horse power. He eventually became an agent for a reaper company based in Lancaster County, Pennsylvania. Perhaps the most important invention in farming between 1830 and 1860, the reaper cut down on the number of men needed to harvest a crop, allowing for more grain production and thus more potential profit.[57] Suter's purchase of a reaper and his marketing of the machines to his neighbors reveals his acceptance of this efficient tool. It would be naive to believe that he did not see the possibility of making money in the venture, and yet, it would be equally incorrect to not recognize the importance of his enthusiastic acceptance of this relatively new time-and-labor-saving device. While reapers had been available before the Civil War, in the early 1870s they became more affordable and were marketed on a much larger scale, and as David B. Danbom observes, of the many nineteenth-century mechanical innovations, "none was more important than the reaper." Farmers using only cradles could cut two or three acres in a day; however, with a reaper that number rose to twelve to fifteen.[58]

Suter's adoption of the reaper indicates his farming acumen. In June of 1870, Suter took time off from turning ware in his shop to visit Harrisonburg "to see about get[t]ing a reaper."[59] Four days later he returned to town to pick up his purchase, and on the fourteenth, Suter noted in his diary that "This afternoon Adam Showalter & myself put up my reaper."[60] The reaper worked to Suter's satisfaction; by January of 1871 he was negotiating to be the company's agent in Rockingham County.

A series of letters from Marsh, Grier & Co. to Emanuel Suter offers an informative look at how farm machinery was disseminated in the nineteenth-century Shenandoah Valley. Revealing that the local representative Adam Showalter no longer wanted the company's agency in the county, Marsh and Grier offer the position to Suter, suggesting that "in relation to commissions &c. will say that we can be as liberal as other partys [*sic*]."[61] In subsequent letters the company proposes that Suter accept a 15 percent commission on his sale of a $190 machine, adding that the regular commission varies from twenty to thirty dollars per sale.[62]

Suter was prepared to sell reapers. On April 20, 1871, he received a note from the company in the handwriting of John Grier, explaining the procedure now that he was in business. Grier wrote: "As the third Monday of April is past there is no need of taking out a license until May 1st. We will bear 1/2 of the expense of the license if you sell but five machines and 2/3 if you sell ten. You can exhibit & not sell the machines until after May 1st as in fact you have no machines to sell—this one is for the present only a sample."[63] A shrewd businessman, Suter wrote back with another proposition. He suggested that he send the company $150.00 for each machine sold and that Marsh and Grier would have no other expenses to cover. The company then agreed and sent him six machines.[64]

By mid-May Suter was actively selling the supplied reapers throughout Rockingham and Augusta counties. Capitalizing on the gathering of a crowd, on May 18th he "went up to George Christman's sale to exhibit my reaper."[65] From that day forward he made a series of visits with the expressed goal of selling reapers:

> This afternoon I went over to Jonas Blossers sold him a reaper. (May 22, 1871)
> This morning I went over to John D. Showalter's sold him a reaper, the Valley Chief. (May 27, 1871)

This morning I went up to the Bank Church to Church meeting then went to the following places. Conrad Sengers for the purpose of selling him a reaper, then went to Simion Heatwoles eat dinner there from thence I went to Lewis Rickerd also to sell him a reaper, from there came home late this evening. (May 29, 1871)

I went out to Joseph Bowmans to sell him a reaper. (June 1, 1871)

Went out to Jonas Blossers he paid me fifteen dollars on a reaper that he bought of me. . . . Then came home, Daniel H. Good gave me one hundred & eighty dollars for a reaper that George Showalter bought of me in Augusta Co. (June 5, 1871)

This morning I went to Harrisonburg helped to load two reapers . . . then went to F. Hess to sell them a reaper. (June 7, 1871)

This morning I went up to Kooglers Sale. Sold a reaper to F. Hess & Son. (June 13, 1871)[66]

Clearly Suter was an active and successful agent for Marsh & Grier. Equally obvious is the fact that there was a call for reaping machines in the Valley. Although Suter appears to have marketed his product successfully, there were, of course, other reapers being sold in the county,[67] further accounting for an increase in the interest of farmers in improving their agricultural profits; an investment of $180 in 1871 was a substantial commitment to the farm.

For unknown reasons Emanuel Suter ended his relationship with Marsh, Grier & Co. in 1872. John Grier wrote that the company was "sorry to hear that you want to give up the agency for the sale of the Valley Chief—but you are your own master."[68] Despite this early retirement from the reaper business, Suter was contacted by Marsh & Comp, successors to John A. Grier, in March of 1876 and asked to once again be an agent for the company.[69] Although he agreed to do this, his approach seems to have changed. Rather than tour about the countryside selling his machine, this time Suter set up his reaper on his own farm and had prospective buyers come there to witness it in action. Marsh and Comp note that "we think your plan a good one to get men to come and see it work."[70] As late as 1878, Suter was receiving enquiries about machines. For instance, E. S. Mitchell wrote that he "would like to have the pamphlet for the reaper and to talk to you in regard to the plow we was talking of."[71]

These descriptions of Suter's involvement with both the thresher and the reaper reveal several aspects about his character, his standing in the community, and the role that region played in the transference of knowledge, in this case, technical matters of farming. It is clear that Suter was not the only person in his area who used threshers or sold reapers; however, that he included himself in that group is essential to understanding his perception of his community role. As a young man attempting to improve his farm's productivity, he adopted the new, more efficient methods of production that rapidly appeared following the Civil War. Rather than rely on traditional manpowered ways of harvesting, he, along with many others, accepted the fact that horsepower and machinery was a better way to manage the farm.[72] His experience in threshing for his neighbors and selling them reapers not only served as an example but also made it clear that he was one member of the community who readily adopted new ideas in agriculture.

The regional connections of the Shenandoah Valley are equally significant. Suter's connections with Garver & Flanagan of Hagerstown, Maryland, and Marsh & Grier of Lancaster County, Pennsylvania, suggest where his confidences lay. Although it may be argued that he found these dealers through their convenient location, there was no compelling reason for him to simply choose them for that reason. As demonstrated, he clearly looked down the Valley when he felt he needed to find something, whether a place of peaceful refuge or a reaper. His connections with Pennsylvania and Maryland served to solidify the consequences of those areas' influence on the Shenandoah Valley. Men like Suter found their inspiration in the mid-Atlantic and implemented their findings on their own farms. Subsequently, other members of the community looked to men with his attitudes to see what the new trends and techniques were and then decided whether or not to adopt them for their own use. In this way we can see a direct effect on the movement of ideas up and down the Valley. Suter looked northward and selected ideas that readily fit into the culture of the Valley, and others made their judgements based on what they saw him and others do. Undoubtedly, similar changes were taking place on the farms of other like-minded farmers throughout the Shenandoah Valley and the rest of the mid-Atlantic states. Examining subscription lists to agricultural publications in the nineteenth-century Northeast, historian Sally McMurry found that "'progressive' farmers . . . served as cultural mediators"; Emanuel Suter's efforts demonstrate this to be true in the Shenandoah Valley as well.[73]

Turning again to Taveau's description of the modern farmer, we find one last clue to Suter's interest in agricultural progress. Taveau suggests that the farmer of the 1870s "must be a *live* man, bold in experiment, frank in conviction, and as free from prejudice as he would wish to be of the plague. In this spirit, let him attend the great agricultural fairs; and, in that magnificent display of modern farm-implement, recognize the triumphs of genius which offers to aid him in overcoming the toil of manual labor."[74] Suter fulfilled this vision of the model farmer, for he visited not only local fairs but the two major fairs of the late nineteenth century: the Centennial Exhibition in 1876 and the World's Columbian Exposition in 1893.

When Emanuel Suter and his son Reuben boarded a Philadelphia-bound train in Harrisonburg in late October of 1876, they were joining millions of others who journeyed to the exhibition billed as "a School for the nation."[75] Suter had travelled throughout the Midwest and Canada following the Civil War, but this trip indubitably introduced him to wonders that he had never imagined. Here, all the world witnessed the great progress the United States had made in its first century of nationhood. Here Suter observed the magnificent Corliss engine sitting in a twelve-acre building, providing the power for the many machines exhibited. With his interest in efficient use of power, Suter might have agreed with the humorist Marietta Holley who wrote that the engine "was enough to run anybody's idees up into majestic heights and run 'em round and round into lofty circles and spears of thought they hadn't never thought of runnin' into before."[76]

Curiously, however, Suter made no mention of any specific features of the Centennial Exhibition in his diary nor in the one extant letter that he wrote to his family from Philadelphia. He spent parts of four days on the Centennial grounds and noted that, on October 26, he "visited the following places. U.S. Mint, Zoological Garden, Fair Mount water works, Philadelphia Pottery."[77] It is no surprise that he took the time to visit one of the many potteries located in the city, for he constantly sought the advice of others in the potting business.[78] He reacted exuberantly to the pottery at the exhibition in a letter to his wife: "Today we were in on the Centennial grounds, all I can say about it [is] all the world seems to be here in a nutshell. I will try & tell you some about it when I come home. We saw a great deal of stone & earthen ware, all kinds of flower vases."[79] Clearly overwhelmed by the entire spectacle, Suter mentions specifically that he examined the pottery on exhibit. A contemporary history of the exhibition records the pottery on display, noting that the American pottery "included excellent white stoneware from Trenton, New Jersey, and some excellent terra-cotta specimens from the same State, and an abundance of rich brownware from Liverpool, Ohio. The collection also contained some fine animal specimens from Phoenixville, Pennsylvania. The Greenwood Pottery Company, of Trenton, New Jersey, showed a small model of a brick pottery, and specimens of the clay in the various stages of manufacture."[80] Fourteen years later, Suter would travel to New Jersey and Ohio seeking knowledge of the latest industry trends when he incorporated his pottery business in the 1890s.

Not surprisingly, in 1893, while visiting his half-brother Christian in Garrett, Indiana, Suter also took the opportunity to visit the World's Columbian Exposition in Chicago. He and Christian spent a whirlwind day at the fair in October, but in one day they must have seen many remarkable accomplishments. Suter's account of the day is characteristically brief: "This morning brother Christian Suter & I took the 2:30 train at Garrett Ind. for Chicago arrived there 9:15 AM. We then eat some breakfast then went to the Fair Grounds on the elevated railroad, spent the day there visited all that we could see to day, after dark we returned to the city the same way that we went there eat supper, then at 9:30 we took the B&O train for the east. I am very tired this evening. The exhibits are grand. Simply wonderful."[81] With Emanuel Suter's interest in machinery, the brothers may have visited the "Palace of Mechanic Arts," a building that displayed among its presentations "The Allis Engine, the Largest in the World—Two Dynamos Each With a Capacity of 10,000 Lights—Ten Engines Averaging 2,000 Horse Power Each."[82]

The Exposition's contemporary historian Benjamin Truman boasted: "No man ever leaves the Machinery Building a bit disappointed. If he surveys all that is to be seen carefully and intelligently he has obtained an amount of information concerning mechanic arts that he had never dreamed of."[83] Henry Adams, on the other hand, took a less ecstatic view of the phenomenal displays of the fair, noting sardonically that, "Education ran riot at Chicago, at least for retarded minds which had never faced in concrete form so many matters of which they were ignorant."[84] By 1893, Suter's mind was anything but limited regarding machinery. As subsequent pages will detail, in 1890 he had razed the pottery shop and kiln on his farm and moved into

Harrisonburg, incorporating the Harrisonburg Steam Pottery Company. This new pottery works combined many of the innovations that Suter had observed in his travels—the word "steam" in the name indicating his pride in the incorporation of engines in the new factory.

Whatever he saw at the Exposition, he was pleased with the experience. Perhaps, like Adams, he "lingered long among the dynamos, for they were new, and they gave to history a new phase."[85] Suter had made a substantial effort to simply visit the fair. Unlike Philadelphia, a day's train ride away, a visit to Chicago represented an investment of time and energy. Although Suter was visiting his brother in Indiana, the trip that they made was not an easy one. Ultimately, the tour emphasizes Suter's interest in progress and in learning more about innovative methods. Robert Rydell, a perceptive historian of World's Fairs, has noted that the Columbian Exposition "served as an exercise in educating the nation on the concept of progress as a *willed* national activity toward a determined, utopian goal."[86] Suter may not have felt a part of a national utopian goal, but he certainly felt that progress could improve one's life.

Suter not only patronized national fairs, he visited and participated in local gatherings as well. Eighteen ninety-two was the initial year for two different fairs in Rockingham County: the Rockingham County Fair and the Spring Fair.[87] Suter attended only the County Fair that year, which was held in the fall; however, in 1893, these local exhibitions seemed to have increased their popularity, particularly the Spring Fair. Advertised as "The Second Annual Farmers' Pic-Nic and Machinery and Stock Exhibit," the Spring Fair was Harrisonburg's answer to the great exhibitions. Along with a band contest and "Match Game of Base Ball," fair-goers could attend the Farmers' Institute, "conducted by leading specialists."[88] The local newspaper's account of the fair gives it a glowing review: "The exhibits of farm machinery, agricultural implements, and labor saving appliances for household purposes are decidedly the most complete of any we have ever seen in the Valley. The leading implement manufacturers of the North and West are represented. . . . There are traction engines, threshers, binders, mowers, plows, rakes, cutting-boxes, harrows, cider mills, and nearly all of the heavier machinery used on the farm."[89]

The emphasis on agriculture and labor-saving implements in this summary exemplifies the value placed on these objects in an agricultural community such as Rockingham County. The report also indicates that the level of acceptance had grown since Emanuel Suter's 1870s forays into the reaper and threshing businesses; this was only the second such fair in the county.

Suter went to the Spring Fair each day, noting in his diary on the opening day that "quite a lot of machinery was on the ground."[90] Like the "modern farmer" of 1875, he was still interested in attending the agricultural fairs, and on this occasion he also participated. Undoubtedly seeing this as an excellent opportunity to advertise, Suter exhibited a selection of the wares of his new Harrisonburg Steam Pottery.[91] Along with the exposure of his company's work, Suter must have enjoyed the experience of presenting the products of his labors at an exhibition of up-to-date machinery and implements.

The introduction of agricultural fairs to Harrisonburg indicates a remarkable move from the days when Emanuel Suter traveled from farm to farm demonstrating reapers. In the twenty years that passed, more farmers accepted the progressive ways of farming, ultimately leading to community acceptance of such methods. Suter played a significant role in such a shift. Perhaps few men in 1870 would have specifically pointed to Emanuel Suter as a progressive farmer, and yet, looking backward from the perspective of the county fairs, it appears that he was. Ideas that he advocated shortly after the Civil War were now commonplace and accepted as standard views. Labor-saving machinery had been important to him from an early date; in 1893, it was a given that such machinery was essential. Suter's views on religious matters, too, were ahead of their time. Although his ideas regarding the choice of ministers were not accepted during his lifetime, many Mennonites did begin to feel as he did on the matter, and the requirements were eventually changed. Sunday schools in the church did become successful and are still held in many Mennonite Churches in the Valley today. Suter's opinions, while not always appreciated at the time, were accepted.

DOMESTIC SPACE

Emanuel Suter's liberal mind also ventured into the realm of his home and the domestic landscape of his property. When he moved to the New Erection land in 1855, Suter and his bride settled into the log I-house that had stood on the site since the early nineteenth century. While the couple lived the rest of their lives in this house, the structure was substantially remodeled in 1874, modernizing many features and changing completely the appearance of the house. The Suter family would no longer present to the world a common log house but would instead exhibit a weather-boarded farmhouse complete with a parlor and sitting room. Writing of early nineteenth-century efforts to modernize, Richard Bushman argues "the aim of vernacular gentility, it seems, was less to incorporate up-to-the-minute fashion than to achieve dignity and respectability," and, in this instance, Emanuel Suter sought to showcase his dwelling in the same way he presented agriculture—up-to-date.[92]

In April of 1874, the Suters began their house renovations, ultimately adding a cellar, a kitchen with a large pantry, and two bedrooms all in a two-story ell addition and remodeling the original downstairs rooms of the house (fig. 3).[93] The house already featured a portico, which was set aside while the refinement of the structure moved forward. Outwardly the house transformed dramatically; the north-facing front of the house was prepared for the ell while the former back of the house became the front where the portico was eventually reattached. Additionally, a white picket fence with gate and stile were added, separating the house yard from the agricultural and work spaces of the farm and establishing, in Bushman's terms, "the zone of domestic refinement."[94]

Local craftsmen transformed the Suter home throughout the summer, nailing on the last shingles in mid-August. While the house exterior presented a completely new look, so too did the interior. The original kitchen with its massive hearth metamorphosed into a parlor, the "crucial characteristic of a refined house," while the next-door room became a sitting room, another culturally significant domestic space.[95] Recalling the house from her early years, Suter granddaughter Mary E. Suter wrote of the parlor in her memoirs: "Emanuel filled in the big fireplace to make it smaller. The woodwork was painted a dark brown and panels were coral and walls were blue. The floor was carpeted wall to wall with beautiful red ingrain carpet. The furniture consisted of a set of six chairs with matching rocker, a love seat, fall-leaf table and an organ."[96] With these accessories and trimmings, the Suter parlor reflected a trend documented in nineteenth-century vernacular homes throughout the United States.[97] The parlor offered the Suter family domestic space free from the business of everyday life, a place where guests and family were entertained and special occasions such as weddings were celebrated.[98] The addition of the organ and manufactured parlor furniture signal the family's desire to achieve the respectability aspired to by many nineteenth-century rural Americans.

• • •

This brief and focused biographical sketch of Emanuel Suter illustrates several points about the nineteenth-century Shenandoah Valley, the many traditional aspects of community life that evolved over the century, and the instrumental roles often played by individuals. Suter's belief in progress and his implementation of it—"be it secular or spiritual"—often served as a model for his neighbors. Naturally, not everyone would accept change; however, the eventual community adoption of many of the ideas that Suter advocated suggests that the number of those who agreed with him were larger than those who did not. That Suter often found inspiration in northern movements and, in some cases, those advocated by federal agencies must also be remembered. His consultation with Pennsylvanians and visits to the major fairs of the century further illustrate his willingness to look beyond his community for advice and inspiration. Clearly Suter applied progressive thoughts in the physically sustaining work of farming as well as the spiritually sustaining beliefs of his religion. The most outstanding example of his implementation of progressive ideas, however, lies in his pottery works. The remainder of this study will look specifically at the inspiration for, and evolution of, his ideas and their manifestation in his pottery business.

Chapter Three

EMANUEL SUTER'S NEW ERECTION SHOPS

Emanuel Suter's diaries recount that during his months as a refugee in Pennsylvania he performed a variety of tasks as he struggled to earn money for food and lodging. He hauled loads of wood, hoop poles, and staves in the area of Mechanicsburg and Lancaster, as well as worked as a farm hand. On January 5, 1865, however, he noted that he traveled to Harrisburg to "see Wilcox the potter about getting a job of work."[1] In February, the Virginian finally went to work for the shop of Cowden and Wilcox "blueing ware and fixing to set a kiln."[2] Suter worked steadily at the shop for the next two months, contributing in a number of ways although never turning ware. He recorded the following tasks: bluing ware, slipping ware, making plats, setting and unloading the kiln, and burning and repairing the kiln. On April 19, he "settled with Cowden the potter."[3] I argue that, despite his brief experience at this shop, Suter's involvement there completely altered his understanding of how a potter could manage his craft and business. His actions upon returning to his Shenandoah Valley home and his subsequent decisions regarding his business demonstrate this change in his outlook.

• • •

While little is known of Emanuel Suter's work before he began his diary in 1864, documentary evidence verifies that there was a pottery on his farm prior to the conflict. Philo Bradley, owner of a Harrisonburg foundry, recorded that in March of 1861, he manufactured for Suter a "shaft and step for [a] mud mill." In May of that year, Bradley also charged Suter for 260 pounds of iron for "frames & doors for potters kiln."[4] Upon his return to Rockingham County in 1865, Suter began to operate his shop with little delay, arriving on the farm on June 10 and commencing work in the shop on August 1, confirming that Suter had an established pottery works on his New Erection farm. Working steadily—he records being in the shop every day during August (except Sundays)—Suter burned a kiln of ware by August 31. He produced a large quantity of ware. For instance, on August 8 he notes that he made one hundred one-gallon pots; given that on many days he records working in the shop all day, his shop, and certainly the kiln, were by no means small. Suter operated this shop until he dismantled the kiln on September 15, 1866. During this period he frequently records in his diary turning over one hundred pots per day before firing a kiln. A substantial shop would be needed in order to store this many pots both before and after firing.[5] Such production also illustrates that Suter was earnest about his work as a potter after the Civil War, continuing his work from before the conflict.

Before razing this earlier kiln and shop, Suter had begun to make plans for a new building and kiln. On August 13, 1866, he wrote that "father and myself were makeing [*sic*] out a draft of my potter shop," and by the 18th of September, three days after taking down the old kiln, he recorded that "we laid off my potter kiln [and] Samuel Shrum and hands commenced working on the kiln."[6] Shrum, a local mason, and his crew worked throughout October building the kiln, which sat on a twelve-foot-square stone foundation and contained two fire boxes, each twelve feet long.[7] Suter also gathered materials for the structure, noting on October 9, for instance, that "Father & myself were cutting some timber for a yoak [*sic*] for the potter kiln," and on November 1 that he traveled to "Harrisonburg after some sheet and strap iron to make doors at the kiln chimney," adding that, "this afternoon we were put[t]ing the frame around the chimney."[8] By the 12th of November, the kiln was ready to be fired, and on the 14th Suter recorded that he "helped Joseph Silber to burn a kiln of ware, burned out this evening at seven o'clock."[9]

With the kiln finished and operational, only the shop needed to be built. The frame, measuring sixty feet by thirty feet, was raised on November 20, but the construction went on for some time; as late as mid-December, Suter was buying "window sash and door lumber."[10] Along with wheels for turning, the two-story structure included a clay shed with a mill for grinding and a clay cellar. For the next twenty-four years, Suter would operate the "New Erection Pottery" on his farm, demonstrating how regionally uncommon techniques and labor management, as well as business connections, could encourage and ultimately change a folk tradition.

Unlike Suter's earlier shop, a photograph of the New Erection Pottery exists (fig. 4).[11] Taken in 1885, the photo shows the kiln, shop, and clay shed, as well as workers in the foreground. The influence of Suter's time spent at the Cowden and Wilcox pottery has been touched on earlier; the effect of the Pennsylvanians' shop and kiln design can be seen in the New Erection structure. A sketch of the Cowden and Wilcox Pottery from 1868 illustrates the distinctive trapezoidal-shaped kiln that is also evident in the New Erection kiln (fig. 5).[12] Distinctly different from the round or bottle-shaped kilns common in most nineteenth-century shops, the distinguishing design of these two kilns verifies Suter's adoption of the Cowden and Wilcox model.

Manufacturing data from 1870 provides a good introduction to the level of work that Suter was involved with just four years after establishing his new pottery.[13] He had invested $1000 in his business, which he operated nine months of the year. His materials at the time of the census were valued at $270 and included eighteen tons of clay, eighty cords of wood, 400 pounds of red lead, and three sacks of salt. His wares were valued at $1900. This represents a significant yield for a potter who operated his shop only nine months of the year. Like most folk potters, Suter relied on his pottery to supplement his earnings as a farmer. As Charles Zug has pointed out regarding North Carolina potters, "traditional pottery was rarely a full-time business. In most instances it was a seasonal activity, one that dovetailed neatly with the natural cycle of planting and harvesting."[14] At this point in his career Suter's operation was traditional: he listed himself in the census as a farmer *and* potter, did not operate his business all year, and had only two employees. In the agricultural census for that year, he listed his farm as having a cash value of $4,500, substantially more than the value of his pottery works.[15]

By 1880, with his business more established, Suter had moved away from the traditionally seasonal nature of pottery and reported that he operated his shop twelve months out of the year.[16] This is in contrast to his cousin and mentor John D. Heatwole who worked his shop only seven months each year. During that year, Suter fired at least fourteen kilns of ware—both earthenware and stoneware—and continued to dig clay, turn, glaze, and sell his pottery throughout the year. At this point in his career, Suter hired more laborers to help him farm as well as operate the pottery. Several of his children also contributed to both aspects of Suter's business. His oldest son, Reuben (b. 1858), worked strictly in the pottery, frequently firing the kilns and selling ware.

Despite the variety of work required to manage a considerable farm and pottery business, Suter seems to have kept his hand in the pottery as much as possible. He dug clay, turned and glazed pots, decorated stoneware, mixed glazes, chopped kiln wood, and set and fired the kiln. He also worked the farm and on many occasions did both in one day. For instance, on June 16, 1880, he noted that "this forenoon we worked in the pottery & this afternoon until it quit raining then we cut wheat until night."[17] Suter worked in both realms throughout that year; however, the longest period he did not work in the shop was in September when he was cutting and sowing. He was occupied in these endeavors from September 7 through the 28th, 1880.

PRODUCTS OF THE NEW ERECTION POTTERY

Emanuel Suter operated at least three different shops at various points in his life and primarily produced utilitarian forms. Early in his career, the biggest distinction in Suter's ware was whether he worked in earthenware or stoneware, for he turned many of the same forms in both mediums. Most surviving pieces from these early years consist of stoneware tableware such as squat, lidded jars, pitchers, and crocks in various sizes, but he also made numerous earthenware forms (figs. 6–8).[18] Although a majority of the surviving examples of Suter's work are stoneware, evidence from his diaries suggests that he burned more earthenware than stoneware at the New Erection Pottery. Billheads from the mid-1880s attest to this concentration, reading "E. Suter & Son, Manufacturers of All Kinds of Earthenware" (fig. 9).[19] Despite this billing during the years at New Erection, Suter rendered many of his forms in both stoneware *and* earthenware.

Citing it as an "unusual" aspect of his pottery, Paul Mullins has suggested that Suter lagged behind other potters in his adherence to earthenware, and in some ways Suter did appear to be behind the times. By the mid-nineteenth century, most potters did burn far more stoneware than earthenware when producing household wares, and, as Mullins has shown in the period from 1866 to 1869, Suter's pottery burned nearly equal numbers of earthenware and stoneware kilns—firing twenty-three kilns during the period with thirteen being earthenware and ten stoneware.[20] In the 1880s Suter turned to earthenware flower pots and drain tile as his major production pieces— ware types that placed him firmly in the camps of the potteries that he emulated, the industrial potteries of Ohio and New Jersey. His production of earthenware, then, did not place him behind the times but instead represents an effort to keep up with them.

Many orders for ware remain in the archival holdings of Suter's papers and provide an accurate list of the types he made. An early post-war listing demonstrates the range of forms available following his return from Pennsylvania, suggesting that he may have been making the same before leaving the Shenandoah Valley in 1864. This "Bill of Ware" is located in the memoranda section of Suter's 1866 diary; it lists pieces that he left with a merchant in Dayton, Virginia, to be sold on commission.

12 Pie dishes	1.00
1 Wash bowl and Pitcher	.75
1 Pound cake Baker	.40
2 Pitchers smallest size	.60
1 Pitcher next to largest	.40
2 Deep dishes next to largest	.84
2 Deep dishes middle size	——
8 Mugs	.50
4 Spittoons two set	.60[21]

For comparison, an 1878 order from J. H. Plecker in Staunton, Virginia, provides a good example of the selection of ware available from Suter twelve years later.

Please fill the following order and deliver the ware as soon as possible, or write me how soon you can. I would order more but in order to get an assortment have to get but a few of each kind in order to make a load. This will make about 225 gals. If you bring me clean sound nice ware, of course I don't ask it for less than 12 1/2 cts per gal.

1 doz	1		gal Butter jars with covers		
1	"	2	"		" " " "
½	"	3	"	"	" " "
½"	4		"	" " " "	
1 ½"	1		"	Milk pans	
1 ½"	1 ½		" " "		
¼	"	1	"	Pitchers	
¼	"	1 ½"	"		
1/2	"	3	"	Straight jars no covers	
½	"	4	" " " " "		
¼	"	3	"	Cream pots, crock shape,	
¼	"	4	"	" " " "	
¼	"	5	"	" " " "	
¼	"	6	"	" " " "	

—Of course all the large ware I want the little side handles that you usually put on.

Plecker added a post script for emphasis: "Of course, none of this ware is to be air tight shaped tops like the covered jars you last brought."[22]

These documents demonstrate the variety of ware that Suter offered merchants, and the specification of shape confirms that Suter made a variety of styles within a given form.[23] For instance, Plecker's insistence on having cream pots that are crock shaped reveals that Suter also made cream pots of another shape. The most important aspect of this letter, however, is its illustration of the variety and utility of Suter's pieces. Each of the types ordered by Plecker was used in most homes in the second half of the nineteenth century, and the simple fact that Suter offered them all reveals much about the nature of his shops. A list of forms found in Suter's orders and accounts includes:

jars
pots

jugs
pans
chambers
pitchers double glazed
spittoons
butter pots
fruit cans

Zug has differentiated the many uses of pottery in the nineteenth century, identifying food storage and preparation as two of the primary functions of the potter's wares and defining the jar as the "ultimate pottery form."[24] Suter's shop made a variety of forms for food storage particularly. Since he worked in both earthenware and stoneware, it is unnecessary except in special instances to differentiate between the two mediums when discussing the use and types of his wares. The jar appears to be the form that Suter made in the most variety of sizes.[25] Ranging from a quarter gallon to ten gallons, Suter made wide-mouthed, small-mouthed, and preserve jars in both earthenware and stoneware, adding lids to pieces in both mediums.

Jars were highly functional and used for many purposes in the nineteenth-century home. Before the widespread use of glass canning jars, ceramic jars served the needs for salting meat and preserving fruits and vegetables. Smaller jars also held goods such as salt, flour, and meal, as well as small portions of meat. Preserve jars with specially shaped lips to facilitate sealing were also produced, often in an attempt to compete with glass jars. Most often sealed with wax, simple flat tin lids fit over these lips, forming a seal. One stoneware example bearing Suter's half-gallon mark offers a precisely cut inner rim to accept a locking lid. Suter most frequently made half-gallon preserve jars (fig. 10).[26]

Along with jars, Suter made many other forms characteristic of potteries in the nineteenth century. Bills of ware and surviving pieces indicate that Suter's shops manufactured jugs ranging in size from a quarter gallon to five gallons and that he also turned the important wide-mouthed crock, variously referred to in accounts as "pot," "cream pot," and "crock." The most frequently found piece of Suter's ware today, the one-gallon crock was also perhaps the piece he made most often.[27] The obvious use of this form was to hold milk until the cream rose, the wide mouth allowing the cream to be easily skimmed off (fig. 11).[28] The functions of the basic one-gallon crock were many, however, and people used it for preserving, food storage, and frequently, in the fall, for holding their apple butter. Along with the one-gallon size, Suter made quarter, half, one and a half, two, three, and four-gallon sizes of this versatile form. Attesting to the popularity of the one-gallon crock, the McCorkle Brothers of Middlebrook in Augusta County wrote to Suter in 1877: "Send us one load ware with your best terms. We want no jugs, chambers, or 1/2 gal. crocks. We sell more one gallon than any other size but would not object to some 1 1/2 gal."[29]

The Suter potteries produced tableware, although mentions of dishes are rare and confined mostly to the 1860s. For instance, a note in the back of his 1869 diary indicates that "Billy Powl [Powell]" owed the potter for "2 mugs, 1 bake plate, 1 chamber [pot]."[30] Another bill of ware from 1869 lists a variety of dishes, specifying "larger size, second size, third size."[31] Pans and cake pans are also mentioned occasionally; one note specifies a "pound cake baker." The pitcher, however, was the most frequent form of tableware Suter sold. Apparently he made this form primarily in stoneware and in one and two-gallon sizes.[32] An 1867 bill of ware for Ephrim Mitchell does list two earthenware pitchers, but other references to the pitcher form in that medium have not been located. Only a few examples have been found to date.

Although a few small, molded, and decorative earthenware pitchers attributed to the New Erection Pottery exist, these do not seem to have been a major production form of the New Erection shop. In the late 1860s, Suter had used molds for some pieces, perhaps pitchers, but certainly for spittoons.[33] He recorded that Charles Binsfeld (Bensfeldt), a potter who worked in the shop beginning in 1868, had made a spittoon mold in January of 1869 and that in February Binsfeld was again making molds. Suter himself made these articles as well, noting in August of 1867 that he "was modeling spittoons."[34] He also recorded in March 1870 that he sold a "modelled pitcher" to Peter Wanger for 30 cents.[35] Years later in 1890, the potter's son David Irenaeus recorded in his own diary that he had "sold a dandy pitcher and washbowl (glazed with mahogany) to Aunt Margarette."[36] This is a rare and late mention of ware that was most likely molded.

Along with these vessels for food preservation and consumption, Suter produced utilitarian and agricultural objects such as drain tile, stove flues, and flower pots. Suter began producing drain tile in 1870 and did not stop until he opened the Harrisonburg Steam pottery, at which point he also ceased to make earthenware (figs. 12–13).[37] Letters from the 1880s inquiring about tile indicate that those functional agricultural pieces were among his most important forms in terms of sales during this period. Customers as far away as Staunton and Charlottesville, Virginia, ordered tile from Suter, often in substantial amounts, demonstrating his regional reputation as a manufacturer of that form. For instance, a Staunton resident wrote: "Please write me about whether you can furnish me four or five thousand three inch tile and if so at what price. I need the tile right away."[38] Similarly, other orders requiring hundreds of feet of tile support the supposition that Suter produced much of this form.[39] Since the uses of drain tile varied, many people wanted different sizes, and Suter was able to supply the needed variety. The length could change easily, and Suter also offered different diameters ranging from a half inch up to six inches.

The stove flue was another of Suter's functional forms that was available in different sizes (fig. 14).[40] These pieces were flanged tubes used as insulation around metal stove pipes where they entered into a wall. Until the 1890 restructuring of the pottery, Suter manufactured these pieces in earthenware exclusively, producing a variety of sizes, all slightly larger than the stove pipe that needed to fit inside. Sizes measured in inches included 4 × 4, 4 × 6, 5 × 6, 6 × 6, 6 × 9, 12 × 6, 12 × 7.

Another primary type of ware for Suter was the flower pot. He made this form at least as early as 1870, and it, like drain tile, proved to be a consistent seller throughout his career. Identified by the top diameter, orders for Suter's flower pots range from two to twelve inches, and they often included requests for saucers (fig. 15).[41] The smallest of these pots called a "nourisher," a one-inch diameter piece with a hole in the bottom, was used as a starter pot for plants. Orders for these pieces often ranged into the hundreds. In the mid-1880s, when the majority of Suter's ware was earthenware, he received many orders for flower pots, occasionally even for numbers reaching into the thousands. In 1888, Mary J. Baldwin, the president of a Staunton, Virginia, women's college, sent Suter the following note: "Please send me by freight as soon as possible one thousand (1000) 2 inch flower pots. The price is $5.00, I believe."[42]

In the 1880s, Suter began to bill the New Erection Pottery as a manufactory of "All Kinds of Earthenware," which coincides with the increase of flowerpot and drain tile production at the shop. The most notable order for flower pots came near the end of 1886, when Suter received a request for 20,000 pots from the Staunton merchants Freiber and Coiner.[43] In March of that year, Suter had "built a small kiln to burn flower pots in," and when this order came in, he was using it often.[44] Of course, the potter did not supply all of these pots at once; he noted periodically that he packed pots to go to Staunton.[45] He did work consistently at filling this order, however, turning pots Monday through Saturday for nearly three weeks.[46]

In order to fill a request of this size and keep the rest of his wares in stock, Suter enlisted the help of family members and other potters from the area. Along with his sons Reuben, Perry, Swope, Emanuel Jacob, and D. I., Suter also relied on the skills of John D. Heatwole and Isaac Good.[47] Good had already been turning at the pottery, and his accounts demonstrate the type and number of pots that he turned. The chart lists the pots turned by size, measuring them in inches. Since flower pots were the only type of ware that Suter sold by this measurement, it is clear that Good turned flower pots for Suter throughout the year. An examination of this detailed record demonstrates that in the month of September Good turned primarily two-inch pots. From September 9 through October 2, he turned 8,575 two-inch flower pots, achieving his highest total on the eleventh when he completed 571 pieces. Moreover, on Monday following this month-long spurt of two-inch pots, Good began to turn the three-inch size. From October 4 through the nineteenth, he produced 5,154 flower pots of this size. In other words, he had turned 13,729 of the 20,000 needed to fill the bill. The potters typically worked a standard ten-hour day, but in order to complete such a large order Suter expanded his hours and allowed Good to work a night shift. During this period (7 September to 19 October), Good worked two and a half hours each evening, earning an additional twenty-five cents on top of his dollar-a-day wage.[48]

Along with this phenomenal effort by Good, Suter also called on the services of the seasoned professional John D. Heatwole to help him complete this extensive order. Although Heatwole's accounts are not extant, Suter noted in the back of his diary the days that his cousin worked for him. Heading the page "J. D. Heatwole is turning flower pots for me," Suter recorded that the potter turned pots from 21 September to 16 October, earning one dollar a day.[49] With this talented and productive work force, including himself and his sons, Suter was able to complete the Staunton order by November fifth, noting: "This forenoon we packed up flower pots & took them to the depot to go to Staunton[,] the last of the bill for Fellon & Gorman that Freiber & Coyner [*sic*] sold for me."[50]

For the next year, the Suter potters continued to turn high numbers of flower pots and press drain tile while also producing their traditional line of functional wares. In 1888 and 1889, however, Suter began to mention crocks more often and recorded burning small kilns of crocks, flower pots, and tiles and burning more earthenware kilns than stoneware. From 1888 to 1890, the pottery burned at least nineteen earthenware kilns and only five kilns of stoneware. The last kiln burned in New Erection was a stoneware kiln.[51]

As a folk potter, Suter's ware reflected the needs of the community he served; everyday, functional pieces were the norm. Throughout his career, however, he did occasionally manufacture formally decorative pieces, also using molds to make spittoons, pitchers, and bowls.

By 1874, Suter was turning vases of different sizes and having some painted by local artists (fig. 16). He noted in December of that year: "came by Dayton, home late this evening, had stoped [*sic*] in with John Thompson to see those flower vases that he painted for me."[52] John L. Thompson, listed as a painter in the 1870 census, wrote to Suter in April of 1875: "Please send me those vases so that I may paint them before the busy season comes. We ought to have some of them on hand by April Court, and if I don't get them soon I cannot paint them in time. A lady told me today that she wants twelve."[53] Although none of these painted pieces have been identified, several of Suter's vase forms have survived, exhibiting a baluster form, some with handles, made in earthenware.[54]

Another clue to Suter's vases appears in an 1884 note from Sabine Jervis-Edwards suggesting the addition of handles to his vases. Jervis-Edwards, writing from the Rectory in Harrisonburg, included a sketch with her note indicating her improvements on what must surely have been one of Suter's vase forms. Her entire missive reads: "Could you make me at once some vases like the two I purchased but with handles? This or something like this for handles would improve the look of the vases. If I like them I will take many."[55]

Another form that Suter made was a large decorative flowerpot or urn (fig. 17). Only two of these are known to have existed, and it may be that the potter made them only for his own use since the pair is known to have flanked the front walk of the Suter home.[56] The piece reflects much work and demonstrates the influence that manufactories of such decorative ware may have had on Suter's aesthetics.[57] For several days in January of 1887, he noted that he was working on a "flower pot moddle [*sic*]," spending at least one entire day on the piece.[58] Although Suter clearly had the urge to make decorative pieces, his potteries produced primarily utilitarian wares for storage, home, and agricultural uses.

Glazes

Emanuel Suter's New Erection ware corroborates H. E. Comstock's assertion that "glazing was the mainstay of the Valley's earthenware decoration . . . serving as well to make vessels impermeable to liquids."[59] While some of Suter's earthenware is not glazed—primarily flower pots and drain tile—a majority of the ware is glazed either inside only or both inside and outside, or "double-glazed" as Suter termed it. Suter often recorded that he was "grinding glazing," an activity that required pulverizing the raw materials in a glazing mill. A typical mill worked on the principle of mill stones in a grist mill, grinding the materials between two grooved stone surfaces. The ingredients were mixed with water, applied to the unfired pots, and allowed to dry.

Suter undoubtedly learned glazing techniques from both Andrew Coffman and John D. Heatwole, both of whom made glazed earthenware. While in Pennsylvania from 1864 to 1865, Suter noted on March 29, 1865, that he "went to Lancaster City to get some glazing receipts."[60] The 1860 census for Pennsylvania lists seven potters in Lancaster County; however, in Lancaster City three shops were pre-dominant in the business—those of Henry Gast, Conrad Gast, and Henry Ganse.[61] Although Suter did not identify from whom he received the recipes, his partial diary for 1864 and 1865 does include four "receipts" for glazing. The first two read:

> To Make Black Glazing
> Take 8 parts of red lead, 3 parts of iron filings, 3 parts of calcined copper, and 2 part of zaffre. This when fused will produce a brown black. But if wanted a truer color the proportion of zaffre must be increased.

To Make a Shining Black Glaze
Take 100 parts of red lead, 18 parts of flint and 40 parts of manganese

The next two recipes are under the heading "March 29, 1865. Receipts for Glazing ware," corresponding to the date that he reports acquiring the recipes in Lancaster City.

Pot Glazing
Take one measure of lead, one & a half of slip, four hundred pounds of Manganese to one hundred pounds of lead.

Black Glazing
15 pounds of red lead
1 ¼ D[itt]o of Manganese
1 ½ D[itt]o of Clay
D[itt]o of Flint White

Additionally, in the memoranda pages of the second 1865 diary Suter recorded the following glaze recipes:

Bills of Glazing
18 pounds of Albany Slip
15 D[itt]o of red lead
1 D[itt]o of manganese
1 D[itt]o of Salt peter
_____

25 pounds of sand
25 D[itt]o of Albany Slip
25 D[itt]o of Ground glass
25 D[itt]o of litharge
2 D[itt]o of Borax
2 D[itt]o of manganese

Most of Suter's glazed earthenware exhibits the lead-based glaze common throughout the Shenandoah Valley in the nineteenth century. His accounts include numerous orders for red lead throughout the 1860s to the end of the 1880s. In the first half of the century, lead was not always available from merchants, and potters were forced to produce lead oxide from raw materials, firing litharge in a kiln to produce red lead.[62] Known as calcining, the burning of the lead particles created red lead, the form needed for earthenware glazes. In August of 1865, less than two months after his return to Virginia from Pennsylvania, Suter recorded that he was "calsigning lead" and preparing to glaze pots.[63] By January of the next year, however, he purchased lead from the Harrisonburg merchant Samuel Shacklett.[64] Throughout his career the potter continued to purchase red lead from merchants in Harrisonburg, Philadelphia, Pittsburgh, and other cities.[65] In his diary he never mentioned calcining again.

In addition to lead, glazes also required clay to provide the alumina, which kept the molten lead from simply running off the ware during firing. Most potters mixed the same clay used for ware with the lead and other ingredients. Occasionally Suter did note the source of clay specifically dug for glazing, as on May 19, 1876, when he wrote, "went down to Daniel S. Heatwole's hill after some clay to make glazing."[66]

Rockingham County clay, like most earthenware clay, contains iron oxide, which created a flux and also the characteristic black spotting seen on many examples of lead-glazed Valley earthenware. Silica provided the final necessary ingredient in the lead glazes used by Suter and others. Silicon oxide served as a fluxing agent, adding to the amount of silica contained in the clay, which, along with the lead, created the glossy surface of glazed earthenware pieces. Most often flint or sand served the purpose, and Suter notes in numerous diary entries hauling sand from Dry River or other sources. Like other Valley potters, at this point in his career he relied on surrounding natural resources whenever possible. Potters also used manganese to create violet or brown colors and, as the glaze recipes above suggest, in mixtures to produce a black glaze.[67] The frequency of Suter's use of manganese is unclear, but he notes in 1867 that he "went to Harrisonburg after Manganese."[68] Other written references to the substance have not been found.

Decoration

While Suter did, as noted, produce some molded ware in the late 1860s to early 1870s, with few exceptions Suter's earthenware crockery, while most often glazed, is not decorated or formally decorative. The most common ornamental feature of his New Erection ware, both earthenware and stoneware, is three incised lines encircling the widest dimension of the piece. This design element is common among Valley ware, however, and cannot be viewed as distinctive to Suter's work. Much of his work in stoneware exhibits cobalt decoration typical to pottery throughout the nineteenth-century United States. These designs reflect his tutoring from other Rockingham County potters, although he did occasionally introduce new motifs to the region.

Suter's cobalt-decorated stoneware most often features floral designs including flowers with blossoms and, more frequently, simple representations consisting of clusters of three brushed leaves applied symmetrically. On the whole, his work is less individualistic than his mentor Heatwole's and that of other Rockingham County potters such as the sons of Andrew Coffman.[69] Work attributed to Suter's early career, however, exhibits more extensive decoration, reflecting the tutelage of Heatwole.[70] As late as 1879, Suter received orders for decorated pieces: "Sir please don't forget the lids on jars and the flowering and mark."[71] Such requests demonstrate customers' preferences for traditional forms and decorative techniques.

Suter's depictions of birds appear to be limited to chickens, but a three-gallon stoneware churn and a two-gallon stoneware crock demonstrate the potter's imaginatively simple depictions of the common fowl (fig. 18). Although he "painted" ware only briefly at Cowden and Wilcox in 1865, Suter would have gained some experience with the typical cobalt decorative motifs of that manufactory. Numerous examples of the Pennsylvanians' ware feature elaborate depictions of a variety of birds, often applied in the slip-trailing method. Joseph Silber, who also worked at the Harrisburg shop, seems to have carried the bird idea with him to the Shenandoah Valley. His bird silhouette on at least one pitcher is highly reflective of Cowden and Wilcox birds.[72] Compared to both Heatwole and Silber, Suter appears to have spent less effort on decorating his stoneware, preferring perhaps to focus his time on turning ware.

Materials

Clay is the essential material required by potters, and Shenandoah craftsmen were blessed with rich supplies of both earthenware and stoneware clay. Comstock reports that most Valley earthenware clays "are red in color after firing," adding that "in their native states, some are gray to greenish, and in certain areas of the Valley the clay becomes pink or tan after firing."[73] While most of the earthenware clays vitrify at temperatures between 950 and 1,050 degrees Celsius, Valley stoneware clays, containing less iron and more silica, require temperatures in the 1,200 to 1,300 Celsius degree range in order to melt the silica and thus vitrify the ware.

Suter was fortunate in having a source of earthenware clay on his own farm, but he also dug clay from numerous other sites throughout the period of the New Erection shop's operation. Much of his clay came from two areas in western Rockingham County—the Dry River neighborhoods near Clover Hill and Rawley Springs, and the land situated along Muddy Creek in the eastern foothills of Little North Mountain. Additionally, Suter's diaries and accounts indicate that he and his employees mined clay from at least twenty-nine different sites from 1865 to 1890, all primarily in western Rockingham County.

David Hopkins, William B. Hopkins, Lewis Hopkins, Hinton Ralston, and John Ralston, all farmers along Muddy Creek, sold clay to Suter from the 1860s through the 1870s. References in Suter's diary are often not specific, but information pieced together from different resources helps to decipher locations. For instance, in 1865 Suter recorded that he "went up on Muddy Creek to the clay pond," adding this note in the memoranda of the diary: "Clay hauled from D. Hopkins, November 10th, up to this time we hauled 8 loads."[74] This was undoubtedly earthenware clay since during this period Suter mentions glazing ware and "burning out" kilns overnight. Although the potter was not consistent in identifying his sources, he often mentioned the Hopkinses and Ralstons, and also commented that he was hauling clay from Muddy Creek, North Mountain, or John Funk's, another farm in the vicinity. Furthermore, an 1873 account book entry coincides with Suter's diary entry for May 31 of that year. Suter noted that in the morning he "went up to Muddy Creek to dig out some potters clay," which corresponds with the accounting of purchasing "2 loads of clay" from David B. Hopkins recorded in the account book. The same page reveals that four more loads were purchased in August of 1873 while the diaries demonstrate that David Hopkins was a steady supplier of clay throughout the 1870s. Suter paid Hopkins one dollar per load of clay.[75]

Suter's other primary clay source was the land along Dry River, particularly near John D. Heatwole's shop in the vicinity of the Clover Hill and Lilly communities. Having worked early in his career with Heatwole, Suter was certainly aware of the clay deposits in the area, which was also the site of the Erasmus and Lindsay Morris pottery. Just as he often referred to a site merely as Muddy Creek, Suter also frequently noted simply that he was getting clay from Dry River. This could have been mined from any of the following landowners' properties: George Woods, William Berry, George Airy, or Daniel Caricoff's clay pond. Woods, listed in the 1870 census as a farmer, advertised in 1868 that a large deposit of stoneware clay lay on his property, announcing that he would "erect a pottery on the premises."[76] Suter, however, had already used Woods' clay; in June of 1867, he noted he "went up on Dry River to Woodses pond to dig clay."[77] While the exact location of Woods' pond cannot be determined, 1870 census data reveals that he lived along Dry River in the area of Cooper's Mountain, between Lilly and Rawley Springs.[78] Berry's and Caricoff's properties were closer to Lilly, with Berry's land lying along Dry River itself near the Morris pottery. George Airy, who furnished fourteen "4 horse loads of clay" from October to December of 1874, owned property on both sides of Dry River in the vicinity of Rawley Springs and possibly sold Suter clay as early as 1866.[79] In 1874, Suter paid Airy one dollar per load. In the 1880s, Suter also dug earthenware clay on his own land; he frequently recorded helping one or more of his sons or hands haul "up clay from the meadow," and, after five days of work in February of 1889, he noted, "we finished getting up as much as we will need this summer."[80]

In 1879, Suter initiated a decade-long arrangement for purchasing clay from Samuel Hoover, whose lands were located along the north fork of the Shenandoah River near the town of Timberville in northern Rockingham County. Suter had contacted Hoover about his clay deposits in September of that year, and he received the following reply:

Sept. 12, 1879
Mr. Suter,
Sir I ship you today by freight five (5) barrels of the stone ware clay. The agent advise[d] me to buy barrels for to ship the clay in. I hope you can use the barrels. They cost 15 c. a piece. The clay weigh[s] 1855 and 90 off for barrels, 1765 net. I was not with the team myself and the boys did not bring as much as I told them, but I think you will have enough to give it a fair test. Let me hear from you & how it acts.[81]

The experiment was successful: Suter records purchasing clay from Hoover throughout the 1880s. Another note reveals the details of the business deal that the two struck and also describes how Suter began to rely on the rail system in his work, foreshadowing the 1891 relocation of his business along the tracks north of Harrisonburg. Hoover wrote:

> Jan. 6 1880
> Mr. Suter,
> Sir, your card was rec'd some time ago but being away I did not get to answer it until this time. I will load you a car at $3.00 per four horse including the clay & will haul you from 3,500 to 4,000 at a load. I do not know how many loads I could get on a car. It is something that I never done but will try one car at those figures.[82]

For several days at the end of January 1880, Suter records that he was in Timberville at Hoover's place getting out clay. On the twenty-eighth he reported: "Today we were still getting out clay and hauling it to the Depot, finished this evening, then I came up with the train to Harrisonburg, my carload was brought along." At the bottom of the diary page he recorded the costs:

Paid Samuel Hoover for clay	$6.00
For clay & barrels got before	1.50
For pay for boy	.37
Yet due on clay	$12.50

It is unclear if Suter paid the three dollars per load that Hoover suggested or if he paid less, since he and a hand dug the clay. Over the next eleven years the potter purchased at least nine car loads of clay from Hoover, making him the largest clay supplier for the New Erection shop in the 1880s. Although the shipping of clay by rail would become routine for Suter in the 1890s, it was a novelty for both the supplier and the receiver when the arrangement began in 1880.

Along with clay for turning, Suter also mined clay for glazes and dug sand to mix with the clays that he used. In 1876, for instance, he stated that he "went down to Daniel S. Heatwole's hill after some clay to make glazing."[83] He also mined sand from other sites from which he never dug clay. In 1868, he "went up to John Beeries [Beery's] to see about getting some sand to mix with some stoneware clay," and later in the year he "hauled a load of sand out of John P. Good's field."[84] Undoubtedly, Suter mixed sand and clays from different sites to reach the preferred consistency for successfully turning and firing ware. Suter's son Eugene recalled that his father also gathered specific stones at the base of nearby Mole Hill, which he pounded into a powder and used for cobalt decoration on stoneware.[85]

Tools

Apart from his adoption of machinery, which will be covered later, there is little documentation regarding the tools that Suter employed at the New Erection Pottery. Oblique mentions in his diary, however, provide some insight into the tools of his trade. Suter used a potter's wheel, of course, and, although he refers to this essential tool occasionally, he never mentions if he used a kick wheel or a treadle wheel. Comstock theorizes: "Most of the Valley's early potters used a 'kick' wheel," concluding, however, that "later in the nineteenth century potters used the treadle wheel."[86] Suter may have made just such a switch. Notations inside the back cover of his 1864–1865 diary describe measurements for the parts of a treadle wheel.

> Length of spindle 27 inches
> Width of crank 4 ¼
> Diameter of balance wheel 27 or 28 inches
> Eight inches from point to bend in crank[87]

The date suggested by this note coincides with Suter's stint at the Cowden and Wilcox manufactory, and evidence suggests that many Pennsylvania potters used a treadle wheel by the 1860s.[88]

Suter's first direct mention of a wheel comes in 1867, however, when he wrote, "fixed my wheel for turning," but in 1869 he recorded that he "went over to John D. Heatwole's, looked at a potter's wheel."[89] In the subsequent weeks, he and his father were busy fashioning a new wheel for the New Erection shop; by mid-May Suter noted that the two "were making a pattern for a potter's wheel" and on the following day that he continued "working on that pattern for a potter wheel. [And] went to Daniel Heatwole's to get a plank for that wheel."[90] He took his pattern to Harrisonburg "to the foundry to get some or a potter wheel casted" while he and his father were "making a frame for [his] potter wheel."[91] Apparently eager for his new tool, Suter visited the foundry on May 28 and again on June 3, noting that he "went to town after [his] potter wheel but did not get it."[92] The next day, however, he obtained his wheel and then spent June 5 "fixing up [his] potter wheel." Finally successful, on June 6, Suter "finished [his] wheel & turned pots until supper." These are the final mentions of his wheel until 1882, when he simply wrote "To day I was home all day working on my potter wheel &c."[93] At that time, after visiting another craftsman "after a wheel he turned," he again spent two days working on his potter's wheel.[94] Just what the wheel looked like is unknown, but Suter clearly upgraded from his pre-Civil War wheel when he refashioned this essential tool of his craft.

Nineteenth-century potters used a variety of ribs, or shaping tools, to smooth pot exteriors and to add decorative aspects to ware.[95] The concentric lines around many New Erection pieces were most likely made with such a tool, and other ribs may have been employed in forming particular rims or collars. Suter's term for these tools was "scrapers," and on several occasions he noted that he was fashioning these. In 1871, he reported that "this forenoon I was makeing turning scrapers &c," and again in 1893 he noted, "This afternoon I made some turning scrapers."[96] In a more precise reference from 1891, he recalled that while visiting his cottage at Sparkling Springs in the nearby mountains he "sawed laurel to make scrapers for turning ware," offering insight into the type of wood that he may have preferred for such items. Apart from the molds mentioned earlier, Suter apparently did not employ other tools to shape or incise his ware.

Suter's fascination with innovation and progressive thinking spilled over into his pottery works. Certainly the construction of the New Erection shop demonstrates his desire to have what he considered a "modern" and "progressive" pottery. Further adaptations that he made through the years to that shop confirm his inclination to continue improving his production capabilities. Although he incorporated many new ideas into the business, I will focus here primarily on his adoption of a tile press and the change from horse and manpower to steam power as indicative of his willingness to introduce progressive technology into the pottery shop.

In 1866, even before he had taken down his earliest kiln, Suter was improving his ability to increase production by streamlining the glazing process. In February, Suter recorded that he was "makeing arrangements for makeing a glazing machine, this afternoon I went to Harrisonburg after a funnel for the afore said machine."[97] For the next five days, he turned pots, but subsequent diary entries show him returning to his "machine." He reported that "this morning I went to Harrisonburg for the purpose of having a copper spout made for my glazing pump, came home at two, helped Father to fix the pump" and continues: "This afternoon myself and Father finished my glazing machine, in the afternoon glazed pots."[98] Eugene Suter, one of the potter's sons, recalled in 1970 that the "machine" had "a wooden tub in which they mixed the glaze. He used a hand pump with hose and nozzle to spray the inside of the crocks, then dipped them in a bucket of water to prevent the glaze from running."[99] Although there is no further mention of this tool, one can assume that it worked since there are no negative comments either.

Beyond using "machinery" for glazing pots, Suter looked for other ways to increase productivity. By the mid-nineteenth century, drain tiles were gaining widespread use in American agricultural practice as a means of draining excess water from fields, pastures, and orchards. Thus, a utilitarian potter found a ready market if he produced such wares. As noted earlier, Suter seems to have caught on to this idea in 1870, for early in the year he recorded, "To day I fixed for makeing pipe & made pipe, turned some pots this afternoon."[100] For the next two weeks, he notes that he was either "makeing" or "turning" tile as well as pots, occasionally spending an entire day producing tile. In early May, after burning an earthenware kiln, Suter recorded that he and a helper "laid those tile in the drain."[101] From this point on, drain tile became one of Suter's standard forms, and he continually had a call for it.

It is important to keep in mind that Suter used the verb "turn" when he described making tiles, for as time went by he realized the need for a more efficient method of manufacturing these functional pieces. Eight years after first producing drain tile, in July of 1878 he again moved toward modernization, noting that he "made a patron [pattern] for a tile press & took it over to Armentrout's shop [a nearby blacksmith]."[102] By the end of August, the smith had finished his work, and Suter had his press. With a typical low-key response, he noted, "This forenoon I was working at my tile press."[103]

Although he had not invented the machine, Suter was certainly striving for a place on the leading edge of pottery technology by moving from hand throwing to mechanical procedures used by industrial potteries. While other Rockingham County potters continued to work in the traditional manner, Suter persevered in his quest for "progress in all" his endeavors.

Edward Dobson, an early scholar of masonry, has written that there were several ways to make tiles: "Some are moulded flat, and afterwards bent around a wooden core to the proper shape: others are made at once of a curved form by forcing the clay through a *dod* or mould, by mechanical pressure."[104] Suter seems to have adopted the second method. Although he never elaborated on the press he used, in 1883 Suter needed to go "up to Mr. Hatfield to have a rammer turned for our clay press," noting the following day that "he was up at Mr. Hatfield's shop, came home pretty soon then fixed our tile press."[105] Material evidence demonstrates the effect of "ramming" the clay through a press. The inside of tiles from New Erection exhibit extrusion marks while the exteriors are smooth (fig. 19). Recalling his own work in the pottery, Suter's son Eugene remembered in 1970 that the shop's tile press "had an iron plate with a round iron piece attached. Clay pressed on this made a round, hollow tile. Six could be made at one time."[106] The use of such a machine could greatly decrease production time by enabling unskilled workmen to produce more tile in less time.

Another, and perhaps more significant, addition to the New Erection Pottery was the incorporation of steam power for operating the machinery. In December of 1883, Suter either borrowed or bought an engine from a neighbor, noting that he would use it to saw wood.[107] No further mention of an engine is made, however, until late January 1884 when he recorded, "This forenoon I went to town after our line shaft, pullies &c for our pottery."[108] Suter was taking a significant step towards industrialization by integrating this efficient form of motive power into his shop. After installing the engine and line shaft, Suter apparently needed to modify some of his existing equipment. He took his clay mill to a local craftsman for the necessary adjustments, which must have been successful since he noted that "our clay mill works very well, as well as the engine."[109]

Eugene Suter remembered that the engine and line shaft were used to run the clay grinder, wheel, wood plane, saws, and the apple grinder, but since the engine is not mentioned throughout the rest of the year, it is difficult to know to which other aspects of the pottery-making process the engine was applied.[110] An April 1884 notice in Harrisonburg's *Rockingham Register* proudly announces the Suters' new source of motive power: "Messrs. E. Suter & Son, proprietors of the well-known New Erection Pottery, near Harrisonburg, have recently bought and put up in their establishment a first-class engine, and are now making a most superior quality of all kinds of earthenware, which they are selling at the lowest prices. The ware made by these gentlemen is equal to any made anywhere, and we would advise all in need of anything in their line to give them a call."[111] The engine was stationary, not one of the mobile engines often used in farm work. The addition of the line shaft to the pottery shop and evidence from the photograph of the pottery shop prove the engine's location was in the pottery.

In the center of the photograph, near the open door, a flywheel attached to an iron rod with a circular saw blade sits upon wooden frames (fig. 20). The proximity of the flywheel to the shop door strongly suggests that the saw was powered by a belt running from the wheel to the engine inside of the shop. Suter's diary also sheds light on the photograph. In March of 1885, Suter borrowed a circular saw blade from a cousin in order to begin cutting lumber for a house he was building for his son Reuben, noting in April that "Reuben and E. J. [another son] sawed plastering lath," an activity that would continue for another two weeks.[112] The stack of wood in the foreground of the photograph is a stack of thinly sawn plaster lath. Suter's diary lends further support for this interpretation; on March 30, 1885, he recorded that "Reuben raised his house today," and plaster lath would have been a requirement for continuing the house construction.[113] By 1887, Suter was convinced that steam power offered a significant improvement in his works, and on April 1 of that year he sold his engine to Jonas Blosser—the same farmer who had years earlier purchased a reaper from the potter—and replaced it with a newer, more versatile engine. D. I. Suter, another son, noted this change in 1890 when he "helped roll the engine out of the shop to cut up some corn."[114]

The steam engine in the New Erection Pottery suggests several things about Suter's vision of his business. First, as the tile press also indicates, he was interested in labor-saving devices and certainly using steam as motive power answered that need. It is significant, too, that the engine was placed in the shop, identifying it as a tool essentially for the pottery business, not for farm work. If Suter had wanted power for his farm machinery he would have bought a mobile engine. Most importantly, he was demonstrating that his shop was different from the traditional potteries of his colleagues such as Heatwole, Silber, and others. Here we see progress, there the time-tested techniques. Here a businessman adding to his burgeoning enterprise, there a craftsman working by hand. As in other aspects of his life, Suter was keeping pace with the times.

Shop Organization

The New Erection Pottery shop was a 60' × 30' frame building, and, as the photograph indicates, it consisted of two stories with a clay room and cellar on the east end. Another part of the structure, referred to by Suter as the clay mill shed, contained the mill and screens necessary for mixing and cleaning the clay in preparation for turning.[115] Suter noted in April of 1875 that "this forenoon I was fixing to sift sand to mix with earthen ware clay."[116] This task he achieved with two horses that provided the grinding power until the steam engine was introduced in 1884.[117] Suter's diary reveals that at that point in time a smaller mill operated as well. On March 4 Suter wrote, "We also worked at our small clay mill &c," continuing on the following day "helped Reuben at our small clay mill."[118] The shop necessarily housed a wedging table as well, and Suter noted occasionally that one of his sons or an unskilled worker made balls for him, speeding up the turning process and increasing his productivity.[119]

Suter's 1867 diary also provided clues to the layout of the shop. In May he recorded that "we were painting ware and carrying ware in the kiln room."[120] Mary E. Suter, a granddaughter of the potter, recorded in a family history that after the glaze was dry on earthenware "the crocks were carried up two flights of stairs to the kiln," noting that in later years this was the task of the potter's sons who "carried six and eight crocks, three in each hand and one under each arm."[121]

Looking again at the photograph, the small chimney visible on the right most likely serviced a stove in the turning room since the New Erection Pottery operated year-round (fig. 4). Placement of the stove near the wheels and the clay source on the east end of the building helped maintain a working temperature for the clay as well as warmth for the potters. The kiln, located on the opposite end of the shop, would of course provide winter warmth when it was fired. Suter noted prohibitive temperatures just once, in 1893, while operating the Harrisonburg Steam Pottery. Recording that the temperature was only "seven above zero," he tersely commented, "It was too cold to make ware."[122]

Marketing: Sales Range & Techniques

Suter's marketing and sales area offer more insights into the workings of the New Erection pottery. His network of merchants extended throughout Rockingham County but also eventually reached well beyond that area. Several merchants in Harrisonburg sold his ware as did many of the small stores throughout the county, and often patrons came to the shop itself to purchase pieces. With numerous potters in the region, Suter faced competition in terms of the quality of his ware and the price that he could get for a given type—a situation addressed in many letters written to the potter. While Suter did sell his ware locally, by taking advantage of rail transportation he eventually branched out and marketed his products up and down the Shenandoah Valley, even making a small inroad over the mountains to the east selling loads to a merchant in Charlottesville, Virginia. Suter's ability to assure customers at a distance that their sizable orders could be filled was a result of his increasingly year-round production and his adoption of time-saving techniques such as the glazing pump, tile press, and steam engine. By seeking markets along the rail system in the Valley in addition to those accessible by wagon, Suter once again set himself off from the many other traditional potters in the area who confined themselves to a local clientele.

The local community was, of course, Suter's source of customers at the beginning of his career. Numerous letters and notes spanning the 1860s through the 1890s illustrate the lasting relationship Suter had with many of his local associates. His accounts from 1866 to 1868 note "Bills of Ware" sold at the Harrisonburg merchants Samuel Shacklett, Isaac Paul, and Forrer & Clippenger, as well as at Joseph Byrd's in Bridgewater and Lewis J. Smith's in Dayton, towns south of Harrisonburg in Rockingham County. Additionally, Suter's diary and accounts indicate that in the 1860s and early 1870s he furnished ware frequently to his neighbors who stopped by the shop. For instance, in August of 1867, he recorded "To day I was at home waiting on persons that came after ware."[123] Moreover, he wrote similar notes in the following years until 1872. He last mentioned this sales activity in March of 1884. Often these sales detail the needs of the community. For example, in September and October of 1869, Adam Gowl purchased three one-gallon jars, six one-gallon pots, two one-and-a-half-gallon pots, eight one-gallon "earthen" pots, and one half-gallon "earthen" pot. Similarly, in April and August of 1870, Suter furnished the nearby Ewing family with a variety of ware, including earthen and stoneware pots, jugs, jars, chamber pots, a deep dish, and a bowl totaling forty-one pieces.[124]

The potter also advertised occasionally in Harrisonburg's newspaper, the *Rockingham Register*. One September 1875 advertisement declares the works to be in "full tide of successful operation" and lists the shop's offerings as "Stone and Earthenware, of all measures, embracing Milk Crocks, Churns, Jars, Jugs, Milk Pans, Flower Pots, Pitchers, &c, &c." Suter also offered good terms, announcing that "as money is scarce, I am willing to exchange Ware for Country Produce."[125] Following the introduction of the steam engine to his works in 1884, Suter printed an advertisement billing his shop as the New Erection Steam Pottery, Rockingham County, VA. This 1886 document emphasizes Suter's flower pots, saucers, and milk crocks and details prices for purchases by the dozen or per one hundred. Guaranteeing the quality of the goods, the advertisement also states that the ware "will be shipped C.O.D., where contracts otherwise have not been made, as the low prices at which these goods are sold will justify no other course."[126]

Suter established numerous lasting relationships with local merchants from the 1860s through the 1880s. In the early years, ware was nearly always sold on commission with the merchant taking 20 percent of the final sale. Illustrating the state of the economy and the barter system that it relied on, merchants often preferred to take advantage of Suter's 1875 offer and exchange goods (other items which the store might offer) for pots—a less than favorable situation for the potter since he could only use a limited amount of "goods" over a given period of time. As Suter's early advertisement indicates, however, he was willing to operate within this system.

A reluctance to completely adopt this method of exchange may have opened him up to increased competition from other local potters. An example of such a case occurred in 1876 when Suter received the following note from F. M. Stinespring, a store owner in the Singers Glen community a few miles north of the New Erection shop: "I heard from a man that has ware to sell and offers to take half in trade. Now I want more crocks and if you will do this half trade and half money you may bring me 125 gal. crocks earthen ware single glazed. If not please let me hear from you at once. I want the crocks immediately."[127] Suter's reaction is unknown; however, subsequent correspondence and accounts with Stinespring over the years suggests that the two maintained a business relationship.

In other instances, the competition arose from price differences. Numerous notes from merchants recount a kind of price war among local potters; however, Stinespring seems to have been particularly sharp when it came to pitting potter against potter. Less than a month before he sent the above missive, the merchant wrote about Suter's colleague and mentor John D. Heatwole: "Mr. Heatwole is around retailing gallon crocks at 10 ct. He has been here at my door selling at that price. I want to know if he can sell crocks at retail without license. I think he would have to pay tax. He has hurt the sale of your crocks. Please let me hear from you."[128]

Again, in 1878, Stinespring brings a third party into the arena: "I will need more crocks soon. If you can furnish them low as Mr. Sylberts [Silber's] 1 gal. = 8 ct you may bring me 100 gal crocks, 50 1/2 gal."[129] Suter had much competition on the local scene. The number of potters in the area, however, suggests that the market could support them all.

Despite the competition, Suter also found that some merchants considered his ware good enough to command product loyalty. J. W. Minnich of nearby Dale Enterprise wrote: "we will sell all the ware of your make that we have demand for and hope that we may be able to sell a large quantity this fall. We have patronized you altogether in the earthen ware trade, having never bought or traded for a single gallon from any one else though we have been frequently urged to do so by other manufacturers. We did trade once for some stone ware of which I told you, and still have the most of it on hand."[130] This is clearly a testimony to the quality of Suter's work—or at least his prices.

Ware going to merchants like Stinespring, Minnich, and others in Rockingham County was usually sent by wagon and delivered by one of the Suter boys or a hired laborer; however, Suter eventually took advantage of the B & O railroad line through Harrisonburg and expanded his business connections both north and south, venturing as far south as Lexington in Rockbridge County, Virginia, and north to Winchester in Frederick County, Virginia. One of Suter's earliest forays out of his immediate community occurred in 1869, when he offered ware to store owner J. H. Plecker, who was located in Spring Hill, Augusta County—easily a day's trip from New Erection if traveling in a loaded wagon.[131] Apparently Suter felt the trip was worth it, however, and Plecker came to be a valued customer for years to come. Plecker did drive a hard bargain; his correspondence was always straight forward, and he never couched his thoughts in timid language. In his first response to Suter's offer to sell him ware, he made his feelings well known: "I am in receipt of yours informing me you can furnish me ware for goods. . . . I think it no more than right to take some goods from merchants at a distance as well as from merchants close by you. . . . I represent two stores, and the quantity of crocks we will buy certainly ought to induce you to take some goods or I will try and make arrangements with some other kiln."[132] Suter's compliance with Plecker's wishes paid off; records of their dealings stretch into the 1880s, and Suter eventually expanded his contacts in Staunton to at least two other businesses.[133]

Eventually, Reuben Suter became the pottery firm's sales representative, and both he and his father frequently made trips to Staunton to call on Plecker and other merchants. Another incident in the Plecker–Suter relationship including all three participants illustrates the complexities of the pottery business in the nineteenth century and how personalities often entered into the deals. The above note expresses Plecker's business-like attitude, and the following confirms this impression of the man. In a letter to Suter in 1880, Plecker noted that he deducted $1.05 from his payment "for stoneware that leaked which I bought of you two years ago." He continued, noting that these leaks could not be detected until the ware was tested, "which I did myself last summer, trying every piece."[134]

In a rare extant letter from Emanuel Suter to Reuben, dated to the summer Plecker refers to, the potter instructed his son on how to treat the matter. Regarding the reduction of Plecker's payment, Suter wrote: "Make the best settlement you can so as not to give hard thoughts, would rather loos [*sic*] a little than to give offence." He noted in a post script that "he [Plecker] says I said I would make that ware alright. I do not recollect that I said so, for fear of trouble let him take it off."[135] This brief vignette from a fifteen-year business relationship illustrates the importance of treating clients with understanding even if it meant losses in the immediate deal. Suter made many such decisions throughout his career; the range of his selling area suggests that he valued these customers and understood the need to appease their wishes at times.

Suter's attempts to sell ware in Shenandoah and Frederick counties to the north were less successful since he ran into what a cousin referred to as "that Strasburg monopoly," the abundance of potters operating in that town

in the second half of the nineteenth century.[136] Suter did, however, make
the attempt with moderate success. His initial dealings in this area were
with H. M. Baker, a Winchester, Virginia, manufacturer of wheat fans—an
agricultural implement that separated wheat from chaff. Suter seemed more
than willing to swap ware for goods in this case since he felt that he could
use the fan to advantage on his farm. Such a trade would also introduce his
ware to merchants in that area. The potter had initially broached the idea
in the summer of 1875, prompting this reply from Baker: "I made enquiry
of merchants as to what they are paying for first class stoneware and they
are getting ware from Mr. Bell from Strasburg at one shilling per gallon (1
2/3 cts). Did I understand you to ask 20 cts per gallon? The ware is retailed
at 20 cts at stores here (not the Ohio). Now I would like you to have one
of my fans, and I might give you more than Bell gets for his, but could not
allow you the 20 cts as I could not get that for it and would have to trade it
out with the merchants as Bell does."[137]

Diary entries for August 30 and 31 reveal that Suter took advantage of
this opportunity: "This forenoon made two single trees & loaded a load of
stone ware to go to Mr. H M Baker in Winchester Va for a fan. 243 gallons
is the number of gallons sent for a forty dollar fan, 16 2/3 cents per gallon
. . . [at the depot] John Robert & myself loaded in a car 243 gallon stone
ware for H. M. Baker in Winchester for one of [his] wheat fans."[138]

In 1879, Suter and Baker arranged another business deal. Baker wrote on
August 1: "I this day send you one of our full size fans, the same size of the
you got sometime since. . . . Send me about 4 doz jugs, few of them half gallon
and rest in one gallon—don't send any pitchers—and but few large size jars or
crocks—milk crocks and pans—and jars, not large, in fact send me a saleable
bill as you know more about such things than I do."[139] A note attached to the
letter details the ware that the potter sent in reply to the request.

Aug. 11th Furnished on Bill

150	1 gal.	stone crocks
36	1 gal.	stone jugs
1	3 gal.	stone jug
1	2 gal.	stone jug
2	2 gal.	stone jars
10	½ gal.	stone crocks
6		spittoons

Baker responded with a note declaring "I rec'd the ware and it gives entire satisfaction."[140]

This 1879 deal with Baker proved to be beneficial for both parties. Suter received a thirty-four dollar fan and regional advertisement of his ware, and the same was true for Baker, who eventually asked the potter to recommend someone in Rockingham County to serve as an agent for his fans. In December of the year, Baker ordered more ware from Suter, but further requests are not extant. This successful business transaction demonstrates Suter's willingness to relinquish face-to-face, community-based relationships to those that could be conducted through the mail and by rail.[141]

As a result of this venture Suter received an enquiry from a Winchester grocer who had seen Baker's selection of the potter's ware. Although such an instance should be seen as a favorable result of Suter's expansion efforts, his dealings with Lefevre & Company also illustrate a potential problem with the mail-and-rail system with which Suter was experimenting. In August of 1879, two days after Baker received Suter's ware in payment for the fan, the potter received a letter from Lefevre stating that he had seen Baker's assortment and would like an order consisting of "125 1 gal. jars & pots, about 40 1/2 gal. pots & also a small assortment of your other wares."[142] He also requested that they be sent on a sixty-day note.

Suter apparently complied with this order, but by December he had not received payment for the shipment. Corresponding with Baker, Suter asked the fan manufacturer to collect for him. Baker responded by writing that "as for the party you speak of in your letter who you furnished ware to I do not consider them responsible . . . had you written me before you sent them the ware I would have advised you not to send it without the cash."[143] Whether or not payment was received remains unknown; however, these two deals in Winchester illustrate the benefits and pitfalls of a long-distance business relationship. Suter seems to have been encouraged by his expanded business rather than deterred.

These accounts of Suter's interactions demonstrate his navigations through the competitive nineteenth-century Shenandoah Valley pottery world. He faced competition from his neighbors in Rockingham County as well as from the numerous manufacturers in Strasburg in Shenandoah County. For instance, the accounts of J. H. Sonner's shop demonstrate that in the 1880s he sold carloads of ware to Rockingham County merchants

R. C. Sullivan, Basore & Shearer, Kiser & Shutters, J. A. Lowenbach & Son, and Johnson & Kaylor.[144] In spite of this competitive market, Suter consistently guided his ever-expanding business toward the corporate world he would enter in 1891.

Labor

Suter's ability to balance his farm work and keep his pottery business open throughout the year relied on his use of familial and hired labor. Along with his eight sons, all of whom worked in the shop at some point in their lives, Suter employed at least ten other workers at various times (fig. 21). Other area potters such as Heatwole, Silber, and Good occasionally turned ware in the New Erection works, usually during periods when their businesses were out of season. Most of the employees, however, performed less skilled jobs such as digging and grinding clay, grinding glazes, and hauling and chopping kiln wood.[145]

Although at sixty years old in 1870 he was elderly by nineteenth-century standards, Jeremiah Falls worked consistently for Suter beginning in early 1867 through 1871. Listed as a "farm hand" in the 1870 census, Suter's records indicate that he also served as an unskilled laborer in the pottery business. The variety of tasks that he performed include digging and hauling clay, cleaning out the clay pit, grinding and taking clay out of the mill, hauling and splitting kiln wood and carrying it into the kiln room, and helping to draw out (unload) a stone ware kiln. Additionally, he planted, sowed, plowed, made fence, cleaned ditches and ponds, and broke up stones in the lane. Falls' farm-related undertakings enabled Suter to spend more of his time in the shop.

Similarly, Joseph Gaines, an African American farm hand about whom little is known, contributed to various tasks on the Suter farm.[146] Gaines appears as a thirty-two year old laborer in the 1870 census and lived along with his family adjacent to Emanuel Suter. As early as 1869, Gaines was laboring with the Suters, and, by 1871, the potter noted that "Joseph Gaines started with a load of ware to Fishersville in Augusta Co.," a journey that he made at least twice that year.[147] Gaines worked in the shop as well, although there is no mention of him ever turning ware. In February 1873, for instance, Suter states that "Joseph Gaines and myself cleaned up the potter shop &c." Other farm hands who contributed to the work over the years included Dave Hartman, Jim Vint, Dave Whisler, and William Lineweaver.[148]

Apart from Joseph Silber (more about him later), the earliest potter that Suter brought to the works was Charles Binsfeld (Bensfeldt), a Prussian immigrant listed as a potter residing in Mt. Sidney, Augusta County, in the 1870 census. Suter's accounts indicate that in 1868 Binsfeld was working for him as early as October, and in November the potter recorded that he "went with C. W. Binsfeld to see about some clay."[149] Furthermore, accounts for January and February 1869 illustrate the work that Binsfeld did in the pottery. For four days in January he made "zagers" (saggers), taking a break on the twenty-sixth to take "ware out of the kiln." On the twenty-ninth he made a spittoon mold, something he did again on February 2. On the fifth he "cut patterns," on the sixth and eighth he "made molds," and finally on the ninth and tenth he "commenced molding."[150] The last mention of Binsfeld appears in April of 1869, when Suter noted that he "went to C. W. Binsfeld to see him about making some pots."[151] Most likely the hired potter did not come back to New Erection. The 1870 Manufacturing Census records him as a potter in Augusta County's third district, working for himself with 8000 gallons of product on hand along with fifty tons of clay, 600 pounds of lead, and forty cords of wood.[152]

Suter often hired laborers to aid him in the shop until his sons reached an age when they could contribute to the work. Often these were men skilled at turning ware, and they continued to find work at the New Erection Pottery throughout the 1870s and 1880s. One such potter, James Ford (1852- ?), appears to have been an itinerant laborer, hiring himself out at least to Suter and John D. Heatwole. As early as 1870, Suter records that he "went to J. D. Heatwole to see James Ford to hire him."[153] Again, in 1876, Ford worked for Suter periodically. For the period of January 18 through February 19, Ford received $41.60, which also included pay for occasional farm work.

Another potter, John W. Ford (1850–1925), James's older brother, also worked for Suter in 1876, performing a number of jobs along with his work in the pottery.[154] As part of his payment Ford must have been furnished with a place to live, for in July the employer noted that "this forenoon I helped John Ford to load his furniture, he moved up to Dry River to J. D. Heatwole's."[155] This was not the end of Ford's service to Suter, however. He worked for him again over the years, and in 1887 he contracted to work in the pottery from April 12 through the end of September, coming back again for April and May of 1888 and from March 26 to May 9, 1889. He also worked there briefly in 1890. Throughout his time at the New Erection Pottery, he received one dollar a day for this "work in the pottery."[156]

Joseph Silber (1827–1890)

Suter must have made the acquaintance of Joseph Silber while the two worked in the Cowden and Wilcox shop in 1865. Silber's name appears in the back of Suter's diary of that year, identifying him as a potter from Harrisburg, Pennsylvania. This is the first connection with this immigrant potter from Baden, Germany, who eventually made a home in the Shenandoah Valley, working with numerous potters until his death in 1890. Quite matter-of-factly, Suter recorded in his diary on October 19th, 1865, that he "went to Harrisonburg, Joseph Silber came home with me,"[157] beginning a complex chronology of the immigrant's movements in the following few years. In the ensuing months, Silber apparently found a spot working with John D. Heatwole, and the two formed a partnership in early 1866.[158] By the sixth of September of that year, however, Harrisonburg merchant J. L. Sibert was advertising that he had on hand "5,000 gallons of Joseph Silber's Stone Ware of Superior make and finish," suggesting that Silber had set out on his own by that time.[159] In November of that year, Suter recorded that he "helped Joseph Silber to burn a kiln of ware," and Silber continued to work with or at the New Erection Pottery through February of 1867. Implying that Suter and Silber did have a business arrangement, Suter records that in February he helped "J. Silber to draw a kiln of stoneware & to divide it."[160] The next mention of Silber does not appear until October when Suter once again notes "Joseph Silber from Harrisburg came here this evening."[161] Contributing to the impression that Silber was working more as an itinerant potter than as a resident, he reported that he resided in Harrisburg, Pennsylvania, when he married Rockingham County native Nancy Swartz in December of 1867.[162]

Silber does not reappear in Suter's papers until September of 1874 when he "did some turning" in Suter's shop.[163] Having moved south to Highland County, Virginia, in 1871, Silber had returned to Rockingham and again contracted with Suter at the New Erection Pottery.[164] For three days in the middle of October, Suter worked on "a frame for J. Silber's potter wheel," indicating that Suter was making space for Silber in the shop.[165] Further signaling a business association between the two potters, Suter's accounts list credits and debits to both men under the heading "E. Suter & J. Silber Co. 1875." This account page lists numbers and types of ware charged to each potter from January 22 to May 7. Silber continues to appear in Suter's records through June of 1875, when Suter records "Joseph Silber & myself settled today."[166] Silber occurs only two more times in the diaries in 1876 and 1882; on both occasions the entry simply notes that Silber spent the night.

In November of 1876, Silber purchased eight acres of property in Rawley Springs, a community along Dry River in western Rockingham County, where he eventually built his own kiln and shop.[167] This venture met with varied levels of success, and Silber's story becomes one of financial hardship for a potter in the last half of the nineteenth century. In order to settle debts the property was auctioned in 1884, but no reasonable offer was made. It was again listed for sale in August of 1886 at which point auctioneer W. R. Bowman sold the house, lot, and "potter's kiln" to Nancy Silber for $181.[168] Joseph Silber eventually traveled to Strasburg where he worked in the potteries of S. H. Sonner and the Eberly family in 1887 and 1888.[169] Silber died of stomach cancer in December of 1890 and was buried in Rockingham County. With little success, Silber's widow attempted to keep the pottery running after his death. Verifying Nancy Silber's pottery operation, two of the couple's sons, John F. and Joseph W., identified themselves as potters in the Mount Clinton Voter Registers in 1891 and 1896 respectively, as did the couple's nephew Otto Karle, an 1868 immigrant also from Baden. Karle listed himself as a potter in 1881, and he lived with Nancy Silber until her death in 1912.[170]

Isaac Good (1851–1907)

The most thoroughly documented potter to work for Suter through the years was Isaac Good. A neighbor of Suter's, Good undoubtedly learned the craft from him. Although Suter does not mention training Good in his diaries, in March of 1868 he records that "to day Jacob, Isaac Good, Peter Layman, Jeremiah Falls & myself went up to the clay bank to get out clay."[171] Good would have been seventeen years old at the time. The 1870 census lists him as a potter, age nineteen, living with his parents. Suter's entry marks the beginning of a life-long working relationship between the two potters; over the next twenty years Good worked for several extended periods at the

New Erection shop. In May of 1871, Suter notes that he "helped I. Good to set an earthen ware kiln," and later that year he "was grinding clay for Isaac Good" while the young potter "dug clay for [Suter] up at David Hopkins."[172] Additionally, the two potters' account books indicate that Good worked at the New Erection Pottery for parts of 1872, 1873, 1878–1881, 1885, 1886, 1889, and briefly in 1891.

The year 1886 provides a unique look at the relationship between the two potters since both of their accounts are available for comparison. Suter's ledgers usually record that Good worked "1 day in the pottery," noting the amount of credit due at one dollar.[173] Given that Suter worked ten hour days, Good was paid ten cents an hour regardless of the work performed.[174] This is the same rate that Suter paid other workers in the shop throughout this period, suggesting that seasoned turners were not remunerated at a higher rate. For instance, when John D. Heatwole turned pots for Suter in 1886 he received one dollar for a day's work as well. In comparison, Carl Grim earned four dollars per day for turning ware at John H. Sonner's Strasburg shop from 1888 to 1889.[175]

Although Good was not paid according to the number of pots turned, he did keep a record of the pots he threw each day along with their sizes. Simple mathematics from a sample day gives us a clear picture of how much payment Good averaged per pot. On March 19 he turned one hundred and thirty-five seven-inch flower pots, and Suter recorded that he worked a full day. Working at that rate, Good turned thirteen and a half pots per hour, making his earnings per pot 0.74 cents. Of course, that rate would change according to the size and number of pots turned, which may explain why Good was given a flat rate for a day's work. This was not always the arrangement between Suter and Good. In 1878 Suter records that Good "turned 152 1 gallon pots at 1 1/2 ct." earning him $2.28.[176]

The accounts between these men also reveal the barter system used in paying for goods and services. Suter's account faithfully records the days worked, crediting Good with one dollar, and he also notes when he paid Good in some other form, putting this down in the debit column. Suter charged Good for items such as a barrel of flour ($4.75), but he also lists work that he performed *for* Good. For instance, on April 20, Suter charged Good one dollar and fifty cents for "plowing & harrowing lot last week." Suter also settled other accounts for Good, including a payment of $3.09

cash for taxes and a four-dollar doctor's bill. When the two men settled at the end of the year Good had earned $157.60 credit with Suter; he had also run up a debt of $79.99.[177] In the end Suter owed Good $77.61.

Clearly both men benefitted from this arrangement. Suter hired a skilled and experienced craftsman to help in his business, and although he never relinquished his own work in the shop, having an extra man on hand to free his time for farm work or other business was quite a boon for Suter. In this way he was able to maintain both a productive farm—for which he also hired workers—and a successful business. Potters like Good enabled Suter to manufacture pottery year-round, unlike other local potters who stuck to the traditionally seasonal business year.

Good, on the other hand, received a steady wage for his work and enjoyed the luxury of working in the community in which he was raised.[178] He benefitted from Suter's employment by working for a businessman who took care of his workers. Although on a much smaller scale than contemporary industrial giants, Suter did practice a form of paternalism towards his employees. In 1873, shortly after Good had moved to Timberville, Virginia, to operate the old kiln at the Zigler pottery site, Suter reported that he "went up to John D. Heatwole's after a glazing mill for Isaac Good."[179] Two weeks later Suter received a note from Good requesting money that the older potter owed him for previous work: "I would like it if you could send me some money if you have it to spare. I need it very bad now. I can do better with the money then to buy on credit. If you can't send it all try and send $10. If you can do so you will oblige your friend Isaac Good."[180] In 1880 Suter was "fixing up the old log house for Isaac Good," and he spent several days bringing the house into order, including fixing windows and other essential features of the house.[181] Regardless of the reasons, workers like Good could count on a certain amount of help from Suter if needed. For instance, in 1883, while he was in Suter's employ, Good's family lived nearly twenty miles away, a distance he could not feasibly travel each day. On one day Suter noted: "This afternoon I went with Isaac Good over the mountain, took some flour & meat & some other things for him to his family."[182] This combination of steady work, life in a familiar community, and a considerate employer made working for Suter a beneficial job for Good.[183]

Reuben Suter (1858–1931)

Suter's oldest son, Reuben, was naturally the first of "the boys" to contribute in the pottery. By 1871, when he was thirteen years old, Reuben was accompanying his father on trips to dig clay, and in the following year he was hauling ware to town. It was not until 1877, however, that Reuben began to contribute in regular and significant ways to the pottery business. His name begins to appear frequently in the diary, performing tasks such as loading and firing the kiln; in fact, he seems to have taken over the entire responsibility of the kiln. Typical mentions in his father's diary demonstrate Reuben's role: "This morning Reuben set fire to a stone ware kiln. . . . Helped Reuben at the kiln he set fire to an Earthen ware kiln this morning."[184]

His father continued to contribute to all aspects of the job; in fact, this year marks a noticeable increase in mentions of working in the pottery. A representative entry reads: "To day I was turning in the pottery all day, made two hundred one gallon pots."[185] Reuben also put in his first full-time year at the pottery. In 1880 or 1881 Suter appended his son's name onto the business, billing it as "E. Suter and Son." Isaac Good begins to refer to the shop as "Suter & Son" in his accounts of 1881. When he married in 1880, the younger Suter listed his occupation as "potter," and he is similarly listed in the census for that year as a potter. The elder Suter's account books for 1885 and 1886 indicate that during that period Reuben earned one dollar per day for work in the shop, the same rate paid to John D. Heatwole, Isaac Good, and John W. Ford. The son also did more than just physical labor; he also received one dollar for "going to Staunton on business."[186] By 1888, Reuben had moved on to a career in business, partnering with Andrew Dold in an agricultural sales firm in Harrisonburg. His name does appear occasionally in the diaries for helping at New Erection and later at the Harrisonburg Steam Pottery Company.

Suter's Other Sons

Emanuel Suter was not at a loss for family labor, and his younger sons picked up any slack left in the wake of Reuben's departure from the business. By 1888, the potter's middle sons were contributing in key aspects of the pottery business. John Robert (1863–1945), Perry Gabriel (1865–1935), Emanuel Jacob (1868–1947), David Irenaeus (1870–1930), and Peter Swope (1871–1952) each began to play significant roles. Suter's youngest sons Eugene

Clifford (1877–1973) and Charles (1881–1960) also performed appropriate tasks for children. Diary entries for 1888 and 1889 include:

> To day myself & David I. were turning ware all day.[187]
>
> To day myself and two of the boys worked in the pottery all day.[188]
>
> To day myself & Swope set an earthen ware kiln, set fire to it this evening.[189]
>
> To day myself & Swope & the little boys glazed pots & set them in the kiln.[190]
>
> This morning I took some crocks out of the kiln, Emanuel J. took a load to Edom & Linville.[191]
>
> This forenoon I & Eugene glazed pots, Swope & Ireneous [*sic*] put them in the kiln.[192]
>
> To day I worked in the pottery, glazed & turned, the boys set the little kiln & set fire to it, we are burning to night.[193]
>
> To day we worked in the pottery all day, Ireneous [*sic*] & I turned 382 1 [one] gallon crocks.[194]
>
> This afternoon Eugene, Perry & myself put tile in the kiln, finished this evening.[195]

These few of the many references to the Suter boys working in the shop illustrate the broad range of activities to which the sons contributed at the New Erection shop. Clearly, Emanuel Suter was teaching his sons the craft of pottery manufacture. Other references indicate that each of the middle sons were capable of turning ware and firing the kilns.

Suter's fifth son, David Irenaeus, kept a diary for eight months in 1890, offering a unique opportunity for another look at the work one of the Suter sons performed in the New Erection Pottery's last year of operation. His notes elaborate on the often brief entries of his father. When the diary begins, D. I., as he was most often known, was teaching at Noble Center School near Dayton, Rockingham County, Virginia, and was "boarding" at a house next door. He finished teaching on March 14, however, and by the seventeenth he was back on the family farm helping "to haul clay from the meadow."[196] After this he worked consistently in the shop, turning ware—flower pots, flower pot saucers, stove flues—grinding glaze, glazing pots, repairing and stacking ware, firing the kilns, and grinding or wedging balls of clay and storing them in the cellar. D. I.'s mention of kiln firing is important since it details a specific skilled task of which his father seems to have relinquished control. This emphasizes Emanuel Suter's increasing reliance on family and hired labor as he moved toward a "managerial" or corporate position in his business. On April 28, D. I. notes that "this forenoon Charley and myself filled the small kiln with ware. This afternoon I kept the fire up," and on the twenty-ninth he records, "I finished burning the small kiln of ware."[197] Significantly, Emanuel Suter does not record this firing in his diary; it is not coincidental since these were the days that he must have been thinking about incorporating his shop into the Harrisonburg Steam Pottery Company. A revealing comparison of diary entries indicates the father's growing attention to his new venture while he allows his sons and "hands" to operate the New Erection shop.[198] For instance, on May 29, Suter records: "This morning I went to town [to] see a man, a potter from New Jersey about the potting business."[199] D. I. simply writes: "Today I helped to make ware."[200] Again, in June, the elder potter reports, "I went to Harrisonburg on business, a joint stock company organized to run a Steam Stone ware pottery in Harrisonburg,"[201] while his son "helped to grind clay and glazing."[202] One more example illustrates Emanuel Suter moving away from the practical aspects of the craft to the business side of potting. On the thirteenth he "went to Harrisonburg took the train for New Market Station. I went down there in the interest of our pottery we expect to establish at Harrisonburg."[203] On that day D. I. "kept fire under the big kiln and put wood in the shed."[204] These comparisons offer a useful glimpse at Emanuel Suter's world as he relinquished the day-to-day control over activities in his shop and focused on a new and progressive venture in the booming city of Harrisonburg.

• • •

The twenty-five years following Suter's return from Pennsylvania in 1865 are marked by an increasing adoption of time-saving techniques and the expansion of his business. By using hired, skilled labor as well as labor-saving machines, Suter managed to operate his pottery shop year-round, giving him an advantage over his competitors in the local community. His large production and stock also enabled him to expand his markets. Aided by the rail system, Suter branched out, primarily up and down the Valley, opening new outlets for his ware even in areas renowned for their own potteries. This focus on expansion eventually led Suter to close the successful New Erection Pottery in 1890, incorporate his business, and move to the nearby town of Harrisonburg, ending a more than twenty-five year business on the farm in rural Rockingham County.

Chapter Four

THE HARRISONBURG STEAM POTTERY COMPANY

"This relieves me of further trouble with that works."

Emanuel Suter Diary, 10 April 1897

On June 10, 1890, twenty-four years to the day from his arrival back in the Shenandoah Valley following the Civil War, Emanuel Suter "went to Harrisonburg on business, a joint stock company organized to run a Steam Stone ware pottery in Harrisonburg (fig. 22)."[1] Although it was most likely not an anniversary of which he was aware—he did not mention it anyway—the connection is significant symbolically. As the previous chapter has shown, after returning from his stint at the Cowden and Wilcox pottery in 1865, Suter embarked on an ambitious endeavor to reform his pottery works along the lines of the Pennsylvania potters he had encountered. Over the next quarter century his business expanded and his means of production changed, allowing him to shift from the traditionally seasonal craft in which he apprenticed to a year-round business that supplied many Valley merchants and residents with pottery. Suter's decision to incorporate his business forms the last link in his chain of making "progressive" decisions regarding his work. Already beyond the aptitude of local pottery knowledge and techniques, Suter sought to step further out of his community traditions and into the corporate world that was burgeoning in the United States in 1880s and 1890s. When he became president of the Harrisonburg Steam Pottery, he took that step.

The previous chapter focused on Suter's career as a traditional potter in the context of the Shenandoah Valley, illustrating his connections to, and variations from, the community-based folk tradition in which he had learned. As he literally moved off the farm, Suter was acknowledging a move away from the traditional, local community toward the much larger community of the industrial United States. He was not alone; so much of the nation was striving in this direction that the period was eventually labeled by historians as "The Age of Energy," a time to be known as the "Incorporation of America."[2] Emanuel Suter had grown—with the nation— from the small folk community in which he apprenticed to the corporate business community in which he would buy and sell goods throughout the eastern United States.

Although his involvement with the Harrisonburg Steam Pottery was relatively short—seven years—Suter's vision of what this new business should be, and how it could become that, provides an excellent opportunity to explore how one traditional craftsman was affected by industrialism and how he sought to enter into this corporate world. Writing about the term "incorporation," Alan Trachtenberg notes that the meaning goes beyond the level of business enterprise. He feels that the word refers to "a more general process of change, the reorganization of perceptions as well as of enterprise and institutions."[3] Certainly this was true for Suter, and this chapter will examine the "incorporation" of the potter, looking at his motivations and the influences that affected him as well as the changes that he made in his business.

• • •

In the 1890s, the town of Harrisonburg, county seat of Rockingham County, expanded. Investors poured money into development, and the word "boom" was tossed about frequently in the local press. Posing the rhetorical question "Are We Booming?," the editor of the *Rockingham Register* offered his thoughts in 1891. After some rumination about the detrimental aspects of "speculation," the writer concludes, "If increase of population, the establishment of industrial enterprises on a good business footing, with the accessories that accompany substantial growth—if these mark a booming town, then Harrisonburg is booming."[4] The Harrisonburg Land and Improvement

Company was one group that encouraged this town growth. Chartered in 1890, the company sought to "acquire by purchase, lease or otherwise, real and personal estate in Rockingham County, Va. To lay out new towns, make additions to existing towns in said county, divide said real estate into blocks and lots to sell such blocks and lots, and to improve the same by the construction therein of dwellings, stores, factories and other buildings, and by laying out of streets, parks or any other improvements, [and] to sell land, lease said lots so improved."[5]

At an 1890 real estate auction in Harrisonburg, the president of the organization "confidently predicted a period of industrial awakening in the near future" and touted the company's parcel of over 200 lots as the best choice for both businesses and residences.[6] A newspaper advertisement for the event proudly announced a few of the industries that had already agreed to locate on the company's property, including a cannery, four cigar factories, an iron foundry, and the Suter pottery, which would manufacture "Crockery and Tiling, to employ twenty or twenty-five hands."[7] The promise of new industry in a town where the "buildings are of a modern kind, and not eye-sores to the visitors" reflected a growing optimism regarding Harrisonburg's place in a nationwide economy.[8] The once small, insular community of Harrisonburg, for instance, boasted of attracting among other industries a Jones and Laughlin rolling mill from Pittsburgh, Pennsylvania.[9] No longer content to rely on its own local craftsmen, the growing town sought businesses from other parts of the country in order to make its way in the commerce of the nation, not simply the county or even the Shenandoah Valley. As was the case with Suter, sources for ideas were no longer culturally restricted to the Pennsylvania region but extended well beyond that traditional hearth. Like Suter, Harrisonburg sought to keep stride with the nation.

The Harrisonburg Land and Improvement Company had its eye on the pottery business before enticing Emanuel Suter to incorporate and move to its property in Harrisonburg. In February of 1891, a charter was granted to the Virginia Pottery Company, a manufactory constructed on the development company's land along the B & O tracks (fig. 23). Familiar names to Harrisonburg residents appeared on the list of officers of the new pottery venture; C. A. Sprinkel (president) and J. P. Houck (secretary/treasurer) were also on the board of directors of Harrisonburg Land and Improvement Company. The manager and operator of the pottery was

William Sherratt, a potter from Trenton, New Jersey, originally from England, who owned patents on certain pottery machinery that he argued would revolutionize the industry.[10] In May of 1890, Harrisonburg Land and Improvement Company board member Dr. S. K. Cox made the motion that the company "accept the proposition made by Mr. W. W. Sherratt of Trenton, N.J. for the establishment of a pottery of higher grade on one acre of the company's lands, upon the conditions that he furnish the plant with its necessary appliances (now owned jointly by him and Mr. Slack of Trenton, N.J.) valued at $5,000 and proceed at once to erect the necessary buildings."[11]

The Virginia Pottery manufactured molded tea pots, pitchers, spittoons, bowls, and other items, but curiously in May of 1892, the company sold its holdings, including its debts, to the newly chartered Rockingham Pottery Company, which was governed by nearly the same officers as the Virginia Pottery. The company was also expanding; the *Rockingham Register* reported in April of that year that "the Trenton pottery which was brought to Harrisonburg in the summer of 1890, promises to be one of the most important industries of the town," continuing, "a charter is in preparation by which the capital stock is to be increased to $50,000, part of which has been subscribed by parties in New York."[12] The company built another kiln, doubling the output of the pottery, and boasted of numerous orders of ware bound for New York City. A *Rockingham Register* article reporting on the initial firing of the kiln noted that the company "now has two double kilns with a combined capacity of 1200 dozen pieces," adding that the company "expects to erect a third kiln in the near future."[13]

According to the local press, the business was a tremendous success: "There are orders ahead for large quantities of teapots, and a steady demand for the ware even in excess of the present capacity. A proposition was declined last week which would have virtually controlled the output of the plant. It was for 1,000 dozen teapots per week at a fixed price."[14] The offer was declined, however, because the directors sought a higher price for the company's ware. The business suffered an unforeseen setback in October of 1892, however, when William Sherratt died suddenly from heart disease. Production at the pottery stopped immediately, and the business of the Rockingham Pottery Company quickly became a matter for the chancery courts. W. T. Dent, bookkeeper and assistant manager of the pottery, offered his assessment of the manufactory's problems in a deposition given in January of 1893. Initial troubles with inferior clay had led to substandard ware being shipped out to buyers, he stated. Subsequently the pottery failed to make money as the company sought to settle the accounts from these poor sales. Additionally, investment in white ware and a skilled decorator and his materials ended badly when the decorator left the company with only half of the ware finished. Moreover, the manufacture of cuspidors, which the company had begun in its early phases, was a failure and was ultimately abandoned. Attempts at manufacturing yellow ware also proved fruitless and costly and were eventually deserted. Still, after adopting Sherratt's invention and producing only tea and coffee pots, the company seemed to be moving in the direction of financial success. Dent explained that "for some time prior to Mr. Sherratt's death, and the consequent stoppage, we had been making strictly first class ware and could command fair prices from standard trade. . . . I claim, that just at the time of Mr. Sherratt's death and the stoppage, that the pottery was in a better position than it had ever been before to make money."[15] Eventually, the court ordered that the Rockingham Pottery plant be sold at public auction; at the sale the real estate and plant were purchased by the Harrisonburg Land and Trust Company for $6,000.[16] The pottery operated under a number of other configurations for the next decade, none of which matched the promise envisioned in the 1890 boom.[17]

Simultaneously, down the Valley in Strasburg, Virginia, another group of businessmen and potters were organizing a corporation based on both the large number of skilled potters and the rich deposits of clay that had made that town a pottery center for much of the nineteenth century. Chartered in Shenandoah County in 1890, the Strasburg Stone and Earthenware Manufacturing Company planned to "purchase, lease and construct and otherwise acquire all necessary plants, kilns, clay beds, houses, yards, sheds, patents and all and singular the equipments and things necessary or advantageous for the manufacture and sale of stone and earthenware products of every kind and nature whatsoever."[18] Erecting an 80' × 40' building and harnessing steam power, the company opened for operation on February 16, 1891.[19]

Like the Virginia Pottery in Harrisonburg, the Strasburg concern experienced setbacks nearly immediately. Three days after beginning production, the second floor of the factory collapsed under the weight of several days' worth of ware. The venture pressed onward, however, and manufactured a wide variety of ware. Noting that the company produced "glazed fancy ware, earthenware crocks, and stoneware occasionally glazed with Albany slip," H. E. Comstock reports that "so much was turned out that the kilns could not be burned and cleared rapidly enough to accommodate their production."[20] Still, by the end of 1891, the company's financial situation was in turmoil. Stockholders mistrusted the board of directors, and numerous lawsuits were brought against the company. Although it originally offered household ware such as crocks, pitchers, flower pots, stove collars, jars, and jugs, the board of directors switched the focus of the plant to drain tile and brick production to tap into the market created by the building boom in the region. By 1897, however, the company had ceased production altogether, and the venture that sought to "elevate Strasburg's status to the level of Trenton, New Jersey, or Zanesville, Ohio," slipped into history.[21]

• • •

In May of 1890, however, the tribulations of the industrial pottery movement in the Shenandoah Valley lay in the future, and on the twenty-ninth of May Emanuel Suter wrote in his diary that he "went to town [to] see a man, a potter from New Jersey, about the potting business"; official documents reveal that he also appeared before an officer of the court, presenting "a certificate and application in writing for a charter of incorporation in accordance with the laws of Virginia."[22]

Previous chapters have shown that Suter valued progress and that he open-mindedly sought advice from sources beyond his immediate community, whether the matter was religious, agricultural, or technical. Naturally, he applied the same technique to his work for the Harrisonburg Steam Pottery; in 1890 and 1891, he made three trips "in the interest of the pottery." He traveled through West Virginia to the industrial potteries of Ohio, to Pennsylvania, and to stoneware manufactories in New Jersey seeking advice on how to arrange the new shop and kiln and ideas on types of clay and glazes to use. The records of his trips serve to illustrate his move toward "incorporation."

That Suter was eager to get this new pottery venture off the ground is evident in the alacrity with which he set about gathering information from other potteries. A mere week after noting the formation of the company, he left on a trip "west to visit some stone ware potteries in the interest of the Harrisonburg Steam Pottery."[23] On this initial trip he stopped at A. P. Donaghho's pottery in Parkersburg, West Virginia, in route to Zanesville, Ohio, where he encountered the Zanesville Stoneware Factory and Joneses Sewer Pipe Factory.[24] He also visited Roseville, Ohio, noting that there were "quite a number of stone ware potteries" and one flowerpot factory there.[25] On his way back to Virginia, he also stopped at a "large quence [queens] ware pottery" in Wheeling, West Virginia.[26] Fortunately, Suter took notes in a memorandum book during his trip and eventually drew up a written report, which is reproduced here in its entirety.

REPORT OF EMANUEL SUTER'S 1890 TRIP IN THE INTEREST OF THE HARRISONBURG STEAM POTTERY

A visit I made to some stone ware potteries in the [west] in the interest of the Harrisonburg Stone ware company.[27] Came to Parkersburg W.Va. 18th day of June 1890 visited M[r.] A. P. Donaghho & Sons Stone ware pottery found it old st[yle,] grinding clay with horse, useing [*sic*] the common pug mill, turning ware with kicking wheel, useing up draft kiln, set ware in old style, salt glaze most of ware, a beautiful clay in appearance ash color used, dug up at door, said not to be very safe burning. A deposit about 18 feet und[er] sand. They have here two round kilns, size 13 feet diam[eter,] 5 feet 8 inches to shoulder, holds 2000 gallons.

Visited Zanesville Ohio Stone ware pottery June 19th, claim to have the latest improved machinery the most modern s[tyles] & kinds of vessels made, slip all their ware inside & s[ome] of it out side such that is burned inside, use the [Albany] Slip straight. The clay used makes when salt glazed rather a brown color, takes the albany slip well makes a glossy black glaze. Mr. Clark said he could furnish us cla[y] laid down at Harrisonburg at $3 dollars & 75 cents [per] ton. They use it every day, is safe burning. The dow[n] draft kiln is recommended for stoneware burning. S[ize] used at this pottery is 27 feet diameter from out to out, 5 feet to shoulder, diameter inside

20 feet in the clear, nine fire mouths, holds 8,000 gallons. They use [a] muffle kiln here same size which is used for burning all glazed ware, albany slip. Capacity of this pottery per [annum is] 800,000 gallons, make about 500,000, run 3 turning [wheels] & one jigger wheels, with the latter one hand [turned] two boys can make 1000 gallons per day. Drying room [seg]ments size 30 & 40 feet of pipe in panel. Size of pipe 1 inch fixed at end to let condensed steam escape, plumber will understand how to fix that. They use 1000 tons of clay [to] make 500,000 gallons of ware. [For] kilns that hold 7000 gallons they use 300 bushels of coal & takes about one barrel of salt to glaze, they use flash walls inside doorway. The best fire brick they use are the Mt. Savage Md. are the best for fire [ho]les for side walls a cheaper brick will do.

June 21th. Visited Roseville potteries, there are about 20 or 24 in number. Kildow, Williams & McCoy are its largest. They make all kinds & sizes of stone ware. They do not wash their clay, they say to thoroughly grind the clay will [answe]r every purpose. They make the celebrated stew pans [conf]irm for all their ware that it will stand cooking & all kinds of heat that it may be subjected to. Size of their kilns, one 14 feet the other 13, holds in the aggregate about 6,000 gallons. T[here] I met with Austin Lowry mold maker, said would [furnish] anything in that line we may want, gave me a [price] list.

[Also] met here with J. D. H. Parrott clay mill builder he makes the clay mills in use here.[28] For a mill 14 feet circle price [?]5 dollars iron hoops around mill will cost from 25 to 28 [do]llars more, he will deliver on board the cars complete for above price.

Close examination of the details in this report reveal Suter's interests and how he perceived the potteries that he visited. His first stop was in Parkersburg at A. P. Donaghho & Sons Stone Ware Pottery. Donaghho had been manufacturing stoneware in southwestern Pennsylvania and the surrounding areas since 1843, and the Virginia potter would have certainly been aware of this shop's ware as evidenced by the fact that he walked two miles to the shop from the train station.[29] Suter's reaction to this well-established pottery is revealing, particularly in the language that he uses to describe the operation: "found it *old* style, grinding clay with horse, using the *common* pug mill, turning ware with kicking wheel, using up draft kiln, set ware in *old* style, salt glaze most ware [emphasis added]." Suter's use of the words "old" and "common" suggest that he was not impressed. These were methods that he had been using at the New Erection Pottery, and he already understood how such processes worked. He was interested in the more progressive, or "modern," techniques that he would find in Ohio.

When he visited the stoneware pottery at Zanesville, Suter noted the difference between the old and the new. There they had "the latest *improved machinery*, the most *modern* styles & kinds of vessels made, slip all their ware inside & some of it out side such that is burned inside, use the Albany slip straight [emphasis added]."[30] The comparison here is obvious: Suter was looking for the "modern" for his new pottery venture. Expecting to compete in a national market, he wanted his ware to be of a similar style and quality, and he was interested in the "latest" techniques in order to make the Harrisonburg venture "modern."

Along with the machinery used and wares made at these potteries, Suter was intrigued by how the ware was made. As noted above, Donaghho used kick wheels; the Zanesville pottery, however, ran "3 turning [wheels] & one jigger wheels [*sic*], with the latter one hand [turned], two boys can make 1000 gallons per day."[31] Such figures must have encouraged this potter who, even with the aid of an engine, was still turning out 150 to 200 gallons a day.

Suter's final stop was at Roseville, Ohio, where he found nearly twenty-five potteries, Kildow, Williams & McCoy being the largest. Here he met the makers of the "celebrated stew pans" who confirmed that "all their ware . . . will stand cooking & all kind of heat that it may be subjected to." It was at Roseville that Suter also met Austin Lowry, a jigger mold maker who boasted that he could make "anything in that line we may want," and J. D. H. Parrott, a clay mill maker who would also happily furnish the Harrisonburg Steam Pottery with a new mill.

This fact finding trip was clearly successful, for Suter did learn exactly how "modern" potteries were operating. Along with the above types of information, he also noted the size and type of kilns used, number of gallons that could be fired at once, and the types of clay used. These are all matters on which Suter, as president of the Harrisonburg Steam Pottery, would have been required to advise his partners and stock holders when the time came for such decision making.

A second trip, this time to the "north," followed this successful tour only a month later, and although no written report or notes exist to detail this journey, Suter's diary does provide some insight into his travels. Stopping initially in Harrisburg, Pennsylvania, Suter looked up his old employers John W. Cowden and Isaac N. Wilcox, finding that both were no longer in the pottery business. Instead, Suter met Cowden's son, Frederick, who had joined the business in 1867, and owned it outright in 1881 after purchasing Wilcox's share in the company.[32] After observing the younger Cowden fire a kiln at his factory, Suter took the train for Philadelphia. Searching for a stoneware pottery but finding none, he traveled to Trenton, New Jersey, where he visited the Mears Pottery and "was received kindly, came away well satisfied, and learned much."[33] That same evening he arrived in Baltimore, preparing to visit potteries there the following day. Although Suter mentions only that he visited two potteries, business cards in the back of his dairy suggest that those shops were M. Perine & Sons, Manufacturers of Hand and Machine Made Flower Pots, and Edwin Bennett's. No further mention of these Baltimore potters is made in the diaries.

The Perine and Bennett potteries were venerable shops in Baltimore in 1890. Coming from a family of potters, Maulden Perine was an established craftsman in the city in the 1820s, and the longevity of his business can be attributed to the willingness of his sons to adapt to changes in the manufacture of ware and competition from other industries. By 1895, the company manufactured a portion of its offerings in Ohio and adopted the use of jiggers as a means of keeping up in the competitive world of late nineteenth-century industrial potteries.[34] In 1846, after several years of work with his brother in Pittsburgh, Pennsylvania, Edwin Bennett opened a pottery in Baltimore where he produced molded Rockingham ware. Credited with introducing the Rebekah-at-the-Well form, the Bennett Pottery operated until the 1930s.[35]

From August 1890 until his next trip in 1891, Suter was involved with taking down the New Erection shop and kiln and constructing the new facilities in Harrisonburg. By March of 1891, however, he was traveling again. On the thirtieth and thirty-first he was again with Cowden, noting that he was at the pottery "looking around the place for information."[36] The primary goal of this trip, however, was to make connections with purveyors of potters' clay. Suter left Harrisburg and again made his way to New Jersey where he visited several mines: "This morning I went to C. P. Rose clay mine looked at his clay, descended in one [mine] 30 feet deep. Saw the hands at work. From there I went to Otto Ernst another miner, did some business with him then returned to C. P. Rose then to the hotel paid my bill, then went to see Leonard Furman another clay miner. He & I went to the depot to see about freight on clay to Harrisonburg, Va., I then took the train for Seawarn from there I walked to Woodbridge to see P. S. Ryan about his clay."[37] Suter was obviously comparing costs for the type of clay he wanted to use at the Harrisonburg Steam Pottery. Although he did not abandon completely using local clays at the Harrisonburg Steam Pottery, he did use clays from New York and New Jersey extensively.

These three trips on behalf of the Harrisonburg Steam Pottery— made before it opened for business—identify the new type of business that Suter envisioned. Although there was already one industrial pottery in Harrisonburg, Suter understood that its managers took their lead from manufactories in the mid-Atlantic and Midwest regions of the United States, and he went to the same source to find his answers regarding how his pottery should be organized and managed.[38] His visits to the factories in Ohio illustrate his interest in new technologies and kiln designs, and those to the clay mines in New Jersey suggest that he wanted to place himself on the leading edge of clay use as well. It is not surprising that, when convenient, he visited F. H. Cowden, the current operator of the shop that had fired his imagination a quarter century earlier. Consulting with Cowden reassured Suter.

Since no photograph of the pottery is known to exist, documentary and material evidence is all that remains to provide information regarding this operation and how it might have worked (fig. 24).[39] J. R. Lupton's 1891 enthusiastic report to the board of directors of the Harrisonburg Land and Improvement Company offers this description of the company on the eve of its opening:

The Harrisonburg Steam Pottery, which occupies a large three story building, which is one of the handsomest manufactories in the state, is now ready to receive and fill all orders, for stoneware of all descriptions. Mr. Emanuel Suter, the President and General Manager of the Company, which has been formed with a capital of $10,000 has long since proven his ability to conduct this business in a most remunerative and satisfactory manner, and already the wares of the Suter make are widely known throughout the Valley as being of the best quality and character, and now with all the modern machinery with which this immense plant is supplied, we are assured that this industry will be a success beyond all peradventure.[40]

Suter's diaries, letters, and notes also provide a sufficient amount of information to give an accurate analysis of the type and size of kiln used, how the ware was made, and what types of clay were used at the shop.

TECHNOLOGY

The Kiln

When Suter built a kiln in 1866, he hired the local mason Samuel Shrum and his crew to do the work. In 1890, however, he would not rely on local workmen, turning instead to an experienced kiln builder—John Hawthorn of Trenton, New Jersey.[41] Construction of the kiln began in early November of 1890 and continued until February of 1891. Hawthorn brought his own workers with him from New Jersey—another importation at the pottery— and the work proceeded smoothly. The crew received $400 to complete this job, as Suter noted: "This afternoon I went to town to settle with John Hawthorn our kiln builder. We paid him three hundred dollars, we owe him yet one hundred dollars to be paid when the kiln is tested."[42] Unlike the barter and credit system that Suter had participated in as an independent businessman, an incorporated business worked on a payment-for-work-done basis. Apparently the kiln builder and the president of the company had signed a contract with the above stipulations.

John Hawthorn's selection as the kiln builder is a significant factor in Suter's efforts to modernize his works. Hawthorn (1832–1896) had spent most of his professional life as a kiln builder in Trenton, New Jersey. An English immigrant from Staffordshire, Hawthorn was noted as one of the first kiln builders to create a reputation in Trenton and other cities.[43] He was sought after by pottery companies throughout the mid-Atlantic and Midwest. For instance, the *Trenton Times* noted in August 1890 that "John

Hawthorn, the scientific kiln-builder, has the contract for building the new kilns at the Akron O[hio] pottery." Hawthorn's 1894 patent for a kiln design that introduced steam into the firing process may shed light on the Harrisonburg Steam Pottery and its operation (fig. 25).[44]

Hawthorn's 1894 kiln patent reveals the specifics of his idea for incorporating steam into the firing process:

> My invention relates to improvements in that class of kilns which are used for baking pottery, and the object of my invention is to produce a kiln which is of simple construction and is adapted to apply hydrogenous heat to the pottery which is being baked. It is customary to bake the pottery by means of a carbonaceous heat, which causes the biscuit or body portion of the pottery and the glazed portion to be heated with different effects, so that the pottery when completed is crazed or crackled. This is owing to the hard nature of the heat, but by combining hydrogen with the carbonaceous heat so as to generate hydro-carbon gas, a more intense by yet milder heat is produced, which thoroughly bakes the pottery but leaves it perfectly smooth, and moreover, the arrangement which I employ for generating the hydro-carbon gas, and applying it causes a great saving of fuel.[45]

More specifically, the document describes Hawthorn's innovation for infusing steam into the kiln during firing:

> On each side of every fire-box are horizontal openings which form a part of the steam flues . . . and in these openings are held removable pans or drawers in which water is placed to generate steam. . . . The pans are opened so as to receive water from the cocks and this also admits air to the flues so that sufficient oxygen may be provided to combine with the steam and the gases of the coal to form a hydrocarbon gas. . . . The steam and air flow together through the flues and by the time the steam and air have reached the bridge walls, the steam will have become superheated and will be ejected in jets into the rear end of the fire-box, thus mingling with the gases of the coal . . . so that an intense heat is generated and is delivered through the said flues into the baking chamber."[46]

Hawthorn's design, clearly on the vanguard of the industry, may have appealed to Suter and his investors as the most up-to-date kiln available. Suter's diary provides further evidence of the possibility of steam in the Harrisonburg kiln in addition to that of the steam engine. In November of 1891, he recorded that "Reuben & Bragg were putting up steam pipe," continuing two days later by noting that "Reuben finished putting in the steam pipe in the shop this evening."[47] No further evidence indicates that this kiln design was built at the Harrisonburg Steam Pottery; however, contracting with Hawthorn—a man with a national reputation as an innovative kiln designer and builder—further demonstrates Suter's move away from the local, traditional aspects of his craft.

The Harrisonburg kiln itself was a round, down-draft kiln with the chamber measuring eight feet high.[48] Since Hawthorn had also built the kiln at the nearby Virginia Pottery, constructing a second one there in 1892, it is safe to surmise that the Harrisonburg Steam Pottery kiln was similar in appearance (fig. 23). Suter noted the following measurements in a notebook:

> Circum. of kiln
> below 72 feet 8 inches
> above 63 feet[49]

The diameters of the above measurements equal twenty-three feet below and twenty feet above.[50] In a letter to his sister Margaret, Suter wrote, "Mr. Hawthorn will be on the grounds next Monday with all his hands & finish the kiln at once, the stack is up now 40 feet."[51]

A contemporary description of Trenton's kilns sheds further light on the appearance of the Harrisonburg Steam Pottery's kiln. According to historian Charles Binns, the city's kilns were "a compromise between a beehive and a champagne bottle.... The oven proper is inside, and consists of a cylindrical chamber about eighteen feet in diameter. The walls are of hardest fire-brick built fully two feet thick, and are pierced at regular intervals by the fireplaces or mouths. These, of course, open into the interior of the oven, where the flames and fuel gases are conducted upwards by enclosing wall called the 'bag.' The top of the cylinder is domed over and certain outlets are provided for the smoke."[52]

The first kiln was opened on June 29, 1891, and, although it was not perfect, it *apparently* satisfied the potter: "To day we drawed the first kiln out of our new kiln it was an earthen ware kiln, it turned out pretty well, burned most too hard; more broke had it not been burned quite so hard."[53] Evidence from Suter's correspondence with F. H. Cowden suggests that the potter did have concerns about his new kiln. A brief note from Cowden dated June 30, 1891—one day after the opening of the kiln—responded to Suter's apprehensions: "It will be impossible for me to be in Harrisonburg by Wednesday morn [July 1, the next day] as we are very busy here and have made no arrangements about going. Possibly you will be more fortunate with your kiln this time."[54]

Suter had telegrammed Cowden with his request for a visit and, although turned down, he continued to seek the potter's advice. In another letter dated just three days later Cowden responded to another pointed telegram from Suter. The entire missive reads: "I would only close the damper about 8 or 12 inches of the trench opening when salting. If you have trouble getting up heat this time do as follows. Put fire brick up at side of iron doors and keep the cold air from passing over fire[,] always seal it[,] that cold air over fire checks heat[,] break up coal often and keep a good draft below under the fire."[55] Obviously burning a new kiln and using a new heat source, coal, had caused some consternation on Suter's part. Curiously, however, there is no mention in the diary of any trouble with the kiln. Following his initial trial with earthenware, Suter burned two stoneware kilns before he even reacted to the quality of the ware. After drawing the second kiln on July 18, Suter did note that "the ware is turning out well."

This reaction makes Cowden's next letter more perplexing. A week after Suter's favorable remarks on the ware, Cowden wrote the following: "I will come down to your place and direct the burning of your kiln on the following terms viz.[:] you to have good Bituminous or Gas coal (mainly lump coal) and supply the men to do the burning, and you to pay my railroad fare and expenses to and from Harrisonburg and lodge me while there, and if I make a successful burn pay me $20."[56] Suter was obviously concerned with understanding the burning of his kiln and apparently was uncertain about his abilities. His reliance on Cowden's experience, although he was himself a potter with over thirty years of experience, illustrates one of the changes that faced the traditional potter as he moved toward industrialization: new technology and materials meant learning new techniques. Since there is no record that Cowden ever came to Harrisonburg, Suter must have grown increasingly comfortable with his own abilities, no longer feeling the need for the Pennsylvanian's guidance. The next recorded correspondence between the two was in 1895.

The Jigger Wheel

The jigger wheel proved to be another piece of equipment that interested Suter during his travels. Recalling that at Zanesville he found that over 1000 gallons a day could be turned on such a machine, it is not surprising that the potter would feel the need for one in his modern shop. Noting that one of the advantages of the jigger machine was the elimination of a need for skilled turners, Georgeanna H. Greer describes the mechanism as one that "has a large base that revolves when powered by energy . . . and plaster molds of various forms can be placed in this base."[57] Although this device eliminated any personal style that a potter could produce with hand-turned forms, it did speed the process of production and would therefore increase profits.

Suter's interest in a jigger wheel was piqued before the steam pottery was in operation. In September of 1890, the company president received word from Cowden: "If you want them molds I can send them to you at any time. If you are going to run a jigger wheel they will be cheaper than to make them."[58] By January of 1893, with the new pottery in full swing, Suter incorporated this technology into the business. He mentioned the machine without fanfare: "The three boys [Reuben, Perry, Swope] were in town or at the pottery again, started to make ware on the giger [jigger] wheel."[59] Within a few days, Isaac Good, who had begun to work at the steam pottery, was making pots on the wheel, and by March Suter reported that "Isaac Good run the giger wheel all day, we are get[t]ing along very well making ware."[60] Commenting on the impact of technology on his family's traditional pottery operation in late nineteenth-century Rockingham County, Virginia, potter Clinton Coffman remarked in a 1963 interview that he never used molds of any kind, declaring "those molds are called jiggers—the western people got'em, that's what actually put us out of business."[61]

Jiggered ware could also feature impressed decoration since the clay was forced into a plaster mold.[62] Suter's diary records several occasions when Good, or one of the boys, was making molds; however, there is no evidence to suggest that the Harrisonburg Steam Pottery ever manufactured molded, decorative ware. However, Suter's note that Isaac Good was making gallon pots in molds indicates that crockery forms were made.[63] Flower pots, too, required no ornamentation and could thus be produced quickly and efficiently. Suter realized this, for on a trip to Baltimore in 1894 he noted that he looked "after a flower pot machine."[64] He never mentioned that he bought one; however, his enquiry suggests that he continued to look for modern and economical ways of producing pottery.

Products

As noted before, in the 1880s Suter switched his production emphasis from food preservation wares to those that were more agriculturally oriented—tiles and flower pots. Although he continued to serve his clientele by turning jars, jugs, and crocks, Suter began to move into the production of items that he felt were on the cutting edge of the industry. As he remarked in the report of his 1890 trip, Donaggho was "old," Ohio was "modern," and he pointed his business in the direction of the modern. It is not surprising, then, that the Harrisonburg Steam Pottery was billed as "Manufacturers of Stoneware Jugs, Stove Flues, etc.";[65] Suter recognized that successful utilitarian potteries made flower pots, stove flues, and the other useful forms that he already made, and he recognized that they made them in stoneware (fig. 26). Emphasizing the Harrisonburg Steam Pottery Company's products, a published President's Report of the success of the Harrisonburg Land and Improvement Company in 1891 noted that a "large pottery has been built and has already begun work for the manufacture of the more common articles in this line, including stoneware in all varieties."[66] In his attempt to enter the mainstream of the industry, Suter used clay that other industrial potteries did, and he sought regularity in his forms by utilizing a jigger wheel. His flower pots were no longer earthenware pieces but were now standard, jiggered, slip-glazed stoneware pots with the recognizable wide rim and tapered sides (fig. 27). The company's jugs and jars, while still hand-turned, exhibited qualities of mass-produced wares such as the use of Albany slip inside (fig. 28). The hues of this ware are also dramatically different from those of traditional Rockingham County stoneware due to the type of clay used as well as the kiln. A comparison of New Erection and Harrisonburg Steam Pottery pieces illustrates this difference (figs. 8, 28, and 29).

As noted, the first kiln fired at the Harrisonburg Steam Pottery was filled with earthenware. Following his return from New York and New Jersey in April, Suter recorded that "Emanuel Jacob hauled clay in to the pottery" from the old clay shed at New Erection. After setting up the machinery and completing other work around the new business, Suter proudly wrote on May 21, 1891, "this evening I turned the first pot made in the new shop."[67] On June 12 and 13, Suter glazed ware and handled jugs, and by the eighteenth the workers had begun to load the kiln. Suter noted that the employees "filled the kiln with earthenware, will burn as soon as we get the bands on the kiln."[68] By June 24 the crew was burning, and on the following day Suter recorded that "we burned out our first kiln, it is earthenware flower pots &c." By June 27 he "prepared a stone ware kiln for burning next week," finishing on July 1. On June 29 he reported "to day we drawed the first kiln out of our new kiln it was an earthen ware kiln, it turned out pretty well, burned most too hard; more broke had it not been burned quite so hard."[69] While he did not comment on the quality of the first stoneware kiln, he did note after the second stoneware firing that "the ware is turning out quite well."[70] Subsequently the Harrisonburg Steam Pottery fired a stoneware kiln every two weeks.

Still contributing occasionally to ware production—turning, handling, cleaning off—Emanuel Suter recorded the ware he turned at the shop for eighteeen days in 1893. The forms he lists are jars, stove flues, and pots. The jars he turned were remarkably large compared to those recorded in the New Erection era. In January and March he produced ten, eight, six, and five-gallon jars, a dramatic increase in size over his earlier forms—the most common former sizes being one to two-gallon pieces. In the spring months he turned more conventional two and three-gallon pots and jars. Again, in August of 1895, Suter noted that he "turned some five and six gallon jars," and throughout the years he frequently "handled" jars and jugs.[71]

Although Suter himself did not record turning jugs or one gallon crocks, material evidence and bills indicate that these were among the most common forms produced at the Harrisonburg Steam Pottery Company. In June of 1896, for instance, the Mt. Clinton, Virginia, merchant W. E. Long purchased two hundred thirty one-gallon crocks. Material and documentary evidence indicates that this standard crock size was both turned and jiggered. In January of 1893, for instance, "Isaac Good was making gallon pots in moles [molds]."[72] Other forms of housewares produced included bowls, churns, jugs, and pitchers. The extant examples of these wares, jugs in particular, often lack the graceful form of Suter's New Erection work, suggesting that other, less skilled turners were making many of these pieces (fig. 29). As advertised, stove flues were one of the company's most popular forms. Suter recorded turning them at the pottery, and extant bills indicate that they were sold in large quantities. In an 1893 letter to his traveling father, Perry G. Suter wrote, "We are making a lot of stove flues this week," implying a large call for the pieces.[73]

The Harrisonburg Steam Pottery appears to have discontinued the manufacture of drain tile, one of the popular forms at the New Erection Pottery. An 1895 inquiry demonstrates that the call for tile remained consistent: "I would not want any sewer piping unless it was stone. And all so [*sic*] I would want it ten inches in diameter. And I would want about 70 feet of it."[74] In April of that year, however, Suter had purchased 500 feet of sewer pipe from Charles H. Torsch & Brother of Baltimore, Maryland. In his diary he reported that he "went to the depot, attend[ed] to the car load of sewer pipe I order[ed] for Peter Wenger."[75] Later, in 1896, he recorded that he had gone "to town after some sewer pipe I bought of H. N. Whitesel & Bro."[76] These transactions all refer to sewer pipe rather than drain tile, although the two would be interchangeable, and suggest that tile and pipe were produced more cheaply elsewhere.

Materials

The type of clay used presents another element of the pottery business that changed with its incorporation. Understanding that modern pottery no longer exhibited the traditional look of gray, salt-glazed stoneware derived from local Rockingham County clay, Suter began to have clay shipped to Harrisonburg for use in the steam pottery. As we have seen, on his early trips to the west and north he looked into who could furnish him clay and at what price, and in 1890 he asked Cowden's advice on the matter.[77] In 1894, however, he made another journey in the interest of the pottery to look specifically into clay and to sell his wares in eastern cities.

Noting that he had made arrangements to "start tomorrow morning to NY on a business tour in the interest of our pottery," Suter embarked on the journey on April 4, 1894.[78] Eventually meeting with C. P. Rose, who conducted a sightseeing tour of New York City, Suter made arrangements with the dealer in "Stone, Pipe and Yellow-ware Clay" and began his journey south, again stopping in Baltimore and Washington on his way home.[79]

The visit to Rose was not entirely a business trip; Suter seemed to be a tourist rather than strictly a businessman on this particular visit.[80] He had also apparently been using Rose's clay since the opening of the Harrisonburg Steam Pottery, and he had visited the mine in 1890. Another letter from Cowden, dated 1891, also shows that Suter switched from local clay to mined clay much earlier than this 1894 trip. Cowden noted: "I hardly know what to advise you in regard to useing Rose & sons clay but think it would be safer to use Ernst & Furmans mixed with Woodbridge to start with."[81] No records remain detailing any relationship that Suter had with clay mines in New Jersey or elsewhere; however, documents do suggest that he may not have totally abandoned using local sources. W. S. Coffman wrote to Suter in 1895 that he would furnish the potter with clay at fifty cents per ton plus $2.25 per ton for hauling it to Harrisonburg (the trip was fifteen miles one way). Coffman noted that "this is lower than I ever sold it when I shipped to Baltimore," suggesting that his clay represented the quality that potters outside of the region found acceptable.[82]

Marketing

While Suter's 1894 trip to New York, Baltimore, and Washington, DC, seems to have been designed to solidify existing business relationships, he did succeed in selling several orders of ware to a variety of merchants. Obviously interested in expanding his markets well beyond the Shenandoah Valley, as president of the company Suter sought to find buyers in these eastern cities that could easily be reached by rail, bringing the Harrisonburg Steam Pottery up to the level of other industrial potteries in the mid-Atlantic region.

While in New York meeting with Rose, Suter also met with Filbert Smith, a merchant in New York City. During the two days that he was there, Suter succeeded in selling Smith a load of stoneware.[83] Suter's sales venture was off to an auspicious beginning. Leaving New York, he marketed his ware in Baltimore before returning home via Washington. Arriving in Baltimore in the morning, Suter wasted no time in visiting "Mr. Ways at the B & O Central business . . . he is their general freight agent." He then "went to see some whole sale merchants to sell stone ware to them."[84] The following day he visited more merchants and then headed for the capitol city.

Apparently Suter was successful on this trip to Baltimore, for he traveled there again in June of 1894 noting that "my purpose is to sell ware."[85] For four days the potter drummed up business throughout Baltimore and Washington. After listing several loads that he had sold, he enthusiastically recorded on two occasions that "the chances are that I will sell more."[86] Finally, after again visiting merchants in the morning, Suter took the train for Harrisonburg on June 9. Although he was as understated as usual in his diary entries for this business trip, a note of excitement is evident in the confident recording of the probability of selling more ware. Despite the fact that there are no known records of sales in Baltimore and Washington in existence, it seems certain that Suter did deal with merchants in those cities.

From 1894 onward Suter's role seemed to become more that of the president of the company and less the acting business manager; that job, it seems, began to fall to his son Swope. The final diary mention by Suter of any dealings with out-of-state merchants is in February of 1895 when he noted that "Swope and I made calculation of the cost of production of wash tubs that some New York parties want made. We then went down town to attend to business pertaining to them and the interest of the pottery."[87] Just what these tubs were and if and when they were made and shipped is unknown, but their mention suggests that merchants did find Suter's ware to be worth the effort to ship to their cities.

Labor

Suter employed numerous established potters at the Harrisonburg Steam Pottery. Two of his sons, Reuben and John, were on the board of directors of the company, and Reuben also served as treasurer. Additionally, both applied their knowledge as potters to the enterprise. Younger sons Swope and Perry also spent time as turners and managers at the factory. Suter also relied on his protégé Isaac Good, who, as noted, was using the jigger wheel successfully in 1893. According to Good's records, he started work at the Harrisonburg Steam Pottery on July 10, 1891, continuing to work there until at least mid-September of that year. In November of 1891 Suter recorded that he "went up on Dry River to see J. W. Ford who is sick & see about someone to turn jugs for us in our pottery," again counting on the seasoned local potter John Ford for his turning skills.[88] Other experienced turners were hired from outside of the region; however, their identities are mostly unknown. In June of 1891 Suter reported that "a turner from Harrisburg, PA came to day[,] he will turn for us in the pottery," although no further mention of this man was made.[89] The artisan was most likely E. S. Thomas, about whom Cowden had written in September of 1890: "I think Mr. E. S.

Thomas would suit you as a turner, he can make large ware. He has been working at the stoneware business nearly all his life, although it is nearly 20 years since he worked in Hbg [Harrisburg]. I cannot say what he knows about setting and burning, he claims to know all about it."[90]

Ephraim S. Thomas (1838–1895) was, as Cowden suggested, an accomplished potter. In 1855, his father Shem Thomas moved his family to Harrisburg, Pennsylvania, from Penn Yan, New York, where he had operated a stoneware manufactory.[91] Eventually working for John Wallace Cowden and Isaac Wilcox, Thomas introduced his three sons to the business, and in 1870 they opened a pottery in Huntingdon, Pennsylvania. Ephraim left the business in 1874, eventually working for Cowden and Wilcox. By the 1880s he was working for the Des Moines Pottery Works in Iowa, but Harrisburg city directories indicate that he was a resident there in the early 1890s. He may well have come down to Harrisonburg to work in the Harrisonburg Steam Pottery.

Unskilled workers also contributed to the labor force at the Harrisonburg Steam Pottery, and Suter relied on his local networks to find seasonal laborers. Charles N. Burkholder, a young neighbor in his early twenties, Benjamin Franklin Suter, Emanuel Suter's nephew, and another New Erection community member Will Sullivan all worked at the pottery in 1892. Burkholder and Benjamin Suter both left in October to go to school while Sullivan worked for an undetermined time. Perry Suter, writing to his father to inform him of the young men's status, noted that "we are going to let Will Sullivan try burning, I am afraid he will not do as he does not have enough judgment about him for that kind of work."[92] In January of 1897, just months before the sale of the pottery, Suter noted that he had visited the local blacksmith William Berry "to get his son Luther to go in to help at the pottery."[93]

Determining the wages at the Harrisonburg Steam Pottery is difficult. In response to Suter's enquiry, Cowden described his expectations for his turners as well as his pay scale in his second missive of September 1890. He wrote: "I require my turners to have enough ware ready for the kiln when we are ready to set it so as not to delay the setting. I pay about 1 1/2 cts. per gal. for turning, although that is more than most potteries pay. However, I require good work and have good turners."[94] Isaac Good's accounting of his pay, though sparse, offers insight into the payment process at the pottery.

From July 10 through September 12, 1891, he earned $63.25 in cash along with $2.60 in jugs and crocks valued at five cents per gallon. Figuring an accurate pay scale, however, remains a challenge since Good did not record the hours he worked each day and notes several times that he "lost ½ day."[95] Depending on their tasks, workers earned fifty cents to one dollar a day at the Strasburg Steam Pottery during the same period.[96]

CONCLUSIONS

The apparent success of the pottery makes Suter's sudden exit from the company in 1897 perplexing. He played an active role as a potter at the new shop until August of 1895. Up to that date he frequently recorded turning ware, often five, six, and even ten-gallon pieces.[97] His last mention of turning ware reveals no intention of stopping: "I intended to do some turning but I. Good was there turning, I then came home."[98] Oddly, he never again recorded turning ware or even working at the pottery in any other capacity apart from "attending to business."

Perhaps the presidential duties of the company were taking their toll on this life-long potter, preventing him from finding time to practice his craft. After 1895 he frequently recorded being at the pottery, but never referenced turning ware. There was, however, no mention of discontent in his diary, nor is the tone of his writing indicative of such feelings. Regardless of this, in April of 1897, Suter recorded: "This morning I helped to do up the work then I and Swope went to town on some business. Today the Harrisonburg Steam Pottery was sold and bought by O. B. Roller for the sum of two thousand dollars, $2,000, cash. This relieves me of further trouble with that works. We came home at 4 pm then did the work &c."[99]

There is no evidence that the call for ware had diminished or that Suter had any reason for wanting to get out of the business that he had founded just seven years earlier. It has been suggested that administrative problems within the company led to Suter's move; however, there is little evidence to support that theory.[100] Perhaps at the age of sixty-four, after spending well over half of his life in the pottery business, Suter felt that he wanted to retire from the trade. For whatever reason, this once folk potter turned industrialist sold out his stock.

Suter's reaction to selling the business—"This relieves me of further trouble with that works"—is perplexing since the technological advances in his pottery and incorporation were on his own initiative. However, his decision to not reinvest his earnings from the sale of the pottery in another business indicates that he was not interested in continuing his career as a businessman on a national scale. Additionally, the fact that he stopped turning ware two years before he sold out his shares suggests that he may have been ultimately dissatisfied with the new methods of production that he had helped bring to the industry in Harrisonburg.

One aspect of the traditional pottery was carried on at the Harrisonburg Steam Pottery beyond Emanuel Suter, however. In May of 1897, he recorded that his sons Reuben and Swope had contracted to run the pottery. Here the familial tradition of potting was handed down to the next generation, but this passing of the tradition took place in the corporate business world. Suter was no longer affiliated with the company when his sons, whom he had trained, "contracted" to run the business that he had created, a dramatic change from the traditional family potteries that existed for many years throughout the Shenandoah Valley and other regions of the United States.

The Harrisonburg Steam Pottery continued to produce pottery for several more years, but little is known about it after Suter sold out his shares. Throughout the remainder of 1897 and into 1899, he notes that Reuben, John, and Swope continued to work at the pottery, and he was still delivering ware that he sold in the previous year.[101] Facts about the final years of the Harrisonburg Steam Pottery are elusive; however, the June 1902 Sanborn map lists the works as "Not Running." By October of that year the building itself had been sold. As noted in the local newspaper the *Rockingham Register*: "F. L. Sublett has purchased the Suter pottery building on the 'boom' and will have it taken down and rebuilt on the old jail lot on West Market Street, with a frontage on the Valley railroad. The building will be used for general warehouse purposes."[102] Furthermore, a March 1906 deed between O. B. Roller and Jacob A. Neff records that the land conveyed was "part of the same land upon which was formerly located the Harrisonburg Steam Pottery Company."[103]

EPILOGUE

Like many traditional crafts, nineteenth-century folk pottery in the United States was primarily a rural enterprise serving the needs of the surrounding communities. Potters made the ware that neighbors found useful, reliable, and attractive. Traditional crafts were perpetuated by passing knowledge and skills along to family members or other community members in face-to-face communication. This enabled the continuance of community-accepted designs and led to regional folk art styles; the work of Rockingham County potters presents few exceptions. As the century moved forward, beyond the trauma of a civil war, rural qualities and ideals began to shift to a more progressive attitude; Emanuel Suter's approach to the pottery business represents this separation from the traditions of the past.

His use of familial and hired labor did not set him off from the other folk potters in Rockingham County; however, his ability to juggle his farming responsibilities with those of his business, enabling him to keep the pottery running year-round, did separate him from the seasonal nature of the nineteenth-century folk pottery traditions in the Valley. By hiring experienced journeymen and contracting with established potters during their off seasons, Suter moved ahead of his colleagues in thought and practice. Similarly, his adoption of steam power and his quick acceptance of rail transportation as a way of broadening his markets set him apart from the other potters in the county.

Emanuel Suter's 1890 restructuring of his business reflects one regional businessman's reaction to increasing economic opportunities as the Shenandoah Valley broadened its connections with other regions. In fact, the record of Suter's business history illuminates a larger trend in the Valley in the second half of the nineteenth century. In 1851, when Suter was an apprentice potter, Harrisonburg was a small town on the Great Wagon Road. The community relied on its own inhabitants to meet its daily needs; there were local blacksmiths, potters, and shopkeepers. Early residents of Harrisonburg reflected the German and Scots-Irish heritage that their ancestors had carried southward out of Pennsylvania, and much of the culture indicated this background.

As this study documents, Suter also felt these familial connections to the local community and the Pennsylvania hearth region. After learning the craft of pottery from a cousin, Suter provided ware for his local clientele, never venturing far from the community. As rail transportation increased the ease of traveling and marketing, Suter broadened his business ties. No longer bound to the local community, traditional markets and alliances gave way to those of a larger scope. Looking back to Pennsylvania for inspiration, he expanded his business along the lines of the Cowden and Wilcox Pottery of Harrisburg and constructed a new shop that exhibited their influence.

Suter's devotion to the idea of "progress" in all aspects of his life, however, also led him away from the traditional ways of life with which he had grown up. His adoption of labor-saving devices within the pottery shop as well as on his farm demonstrates his desire to maintain not only tradition but also a higher level of achievement in his work. Like the "modern farmer" that the commissioner of agriculture exhorted his countrymen to be, Suter strived to incorporate the latest technology into his life. Similarly, in his religious activities Suter looked for innovation and progress. Hoping to modernize the Mennonite Church, he argued for reform, and his arguments were eventually accepted.

By attending the two great fairs of his generation—the Centennial Exhibition and the World's Columbian Exposition—Suter also demonstrated his interest in understanding how the world outside of his community was progressing. Often, as in the case of the mechanical reaper, he modeled that knowledge to the local community. In his hands, the traditional craft of potting reflected increasingly the trends of American culture—a growing acceptance of technology. His incorporation of labor-saving machinery and steam as a motive power moved him out of the realm of tradition into that of industrialization.

Eventually, Suter went well beyond even the traditional ties that he had with the Pennsylvania culture region, venturing into states where the most modern potteries were operating—New Jersey and Ohio. When he designed the Harrisonburg Steam Pottery, for instance, he did not emulate the Pennsylvania potter Cowden but instead hired a Trenton, New Jersey, kiln builder for the task. His wares, too, demonstrate a move toward the industrial potteries of the mid-Atlantic and Midwest as he increasingly concentrated his efforts on flower pots and drain tile and produced comparatively fewer household wares. By the end of his career, Suter had moved well beyond the traditional craft in which he learned and entered into the competitive industrial world of late nineteenth-century pottery manufacturing. This potter's career illustrates the process of the evolution of tradition in the Shenandoah Valley in the second half of the nineteenth century as transportation, technology, and communications increased the ability of craftspeople to interact with regions outside of their local communities.

The Shenandoah Valley's ties to the North, it appeared, were assets that would allow it to branch out into national systems of commerce, but these necessary connections with other regions ultimately became a hindrance. Despite the cultural hearth influence from the north, industrial ventures in the South could not exist independently of northern resources and markets. Suter was dependent upon clay from New Jersey, coal from Pennsylvania, and merchants from New York, Baltimore, and Washington, DC. Other industrial endeavors in Harrisonburg never materialized or failed; the Virginia pottery, J & L Steel, and others lasted only a few years or were never built.[1] D. W. Meinig has reflected that when industrial systems such as that of the mid-Atlantic are developed, "subsequent major industrial complexes are not likely to be independent of it but, rather, extensions from it, bound to it for many essentials even if operated by local corporations." He adds that "there was no possibility of the South nurturing an industrial region at all comparable to that of the Northeast."[2] The Shenandoah Valley, a cultural and industrial extension of the mid-Atlantic region, was never able to become independent of its hearth and therefore never succeeded in becoming the industrial center of which end-of-the-century entrepreneurs had dreamed. Emanuel Suter's story presents a useful case study of how this development played out in a cultural region.

Suter was not alone in this movement; businessmen in Harrisonburg were designing a different vision for Rockingham County even as Suter razed his pre-war shop and constructed the New Erection Pottery.[3] The editor of the *Old Commonwealth*, a Harrisonburg newspaper, expressed his view of such change shortly after the end of the Civil War, reflecting in November of 1865 on the change that he foresaw: "On Sunday evening another of the old landmarks succumbed to the persistent efforts of Young America, whose bump of destructiveness seems to be swelling to extraordinary dimensions at this time. The old church upon the hill, after standing siege, which began at an early hour, until 4 o'clock, tumbled with a crash."[4] "Young America" was clearly on the rise, and Suter's actions indicate that he, too, thought the old ways could be left behind and new innovations used to great advantage. Importantly, in primarily rural and conservative Rockingham County, Virginia, however, Emanuel Suter was the sole proponent of such change in the long tradition of folk pottery production. His venture into the corporate ceramic world *was* successful, but the returns were perhaps not enough to justify his efforts. As he stated, he felt relieved when he stepped away from the business. For the remaining five years of his life he continued to farm, maintaining his progressive outlook by experimenting with grafting fruit trees in his large orchard until his death on December 16, 1902.

Suter's efforts to modernize pottery production in his region represent the most reasonable choice a potter could make if he wanted to continue in the business. Ware produced in the factories of Ohio and New Jersey could be shipped cheaply by rail into the Shenandoah Valley, and it was increasingly available in stores and markets. Suter's recognition that mechanization lowered costs reflected both his precept to value progress as well as his business acumen. Although the New Erection Pottery continued to experience high demand for its agricultural ware, the traditional world of the Shenandoah Valley folk potter was dwindling by 1891 when Suter decided to incorporate and attempt to enter the markets of the eastern cities. John D. Heatwole, while identified as a potter in an 1890 court deposition, had ceased producing ware by 1895.[5] The Coffman family's business declined as the "western people," utilizing jigger wheels, put them out of business. Isaac Good, one of the younger generation of potters, struggled to maintain his craft at the Harrisonburg Steam Pottery and the Trenton-influenced factory in Harrisonburg, but he, too, eventually relied on farming to earn a living, dying at the age of fifty-six in 1907. Joseph Silber, a talented potter who settled in Rockingham County, faced the hardships of a diminishing market for traditional ware in the 1880s, and, after working as an itinerant potter, succumbed to stomach cancer in 1890.[6] The world of the traditional potter was ending, and only Emanuel Suter took a bold step toward sustaining the once thriving craft. His story, then, offers a valuable view into the shifting world of a Shenandoah Valley craftsman in the second half of the nineteenth century.

FIG. I. TWO OF EMANUEL SUTER'S EARLIEST PIECES OF STONEWARE (CENTER AND RIGHT) ALONGSIDE ONE BY SUTER'S MENTOR JOHN D. HEATWOLE (LEFT). PHOTOGRAPH BY WILLIAM MCGUFFIN. COURTESY OF THE HARRISONBURG-ROCKINGHAM HISTORICAL SOCIETY, DAYTON, VIRGINIA.

FIG. 2. ELIZABETH SWOPE SUTER AND EMANUEL SUTER, 1855. PRIVATE COLLECTION.

FIG. 3. THE EMANUEL AND ELIZABETH SUTER HOME AFTER THE 1874 REMODELING.
COURTESY OF THE VIRGINIA MENNONITE CONFERENCE ARCHIVE.

FIG. 4. THE NEW ERECTION POTTERY, 1885. THIS IS A HAND-TINTED
VERSION OF A BLACK-AND-WHITE ORIGINAL IMAGE. COURTESY OF THE
VIRGINIA MENNONITE CONFERENCE ARCHIVE.

FIG. 5. COWDEN AND WILCOX POTTERY, HARRISBURG,
PENNSYLVANIA. PENNSYLVANIA STATE ARCHIVES, MG-
214.1 WARREN J. HARDER COLLECTION, HARRISBURG
AREA SUBJECT FILE.

FIG. 6. THREE EXAMPLES OF EMANUEL SUTER'S SMALL STORAGE JARS ALONG WITH
THE COPPER STENCIL HE USED TO "SIGN" THE MIDDLE EXAMPLE. PHOTOGRAPH BY
WILLIAM MCGUFFIN. COURTESY OF THE HARRISONBURG-ROCKINGHAM HISTORICAL
SOCIETY, DAYTON, VIRGINIA.

FIG. 7. EXAMPLES OF EMANUEL SUTER'S EARTHENWARE CROCK FORMS RANGING
IN SIZE FROM A QUARTER GALLON TO ONE-AND-A-HALF GALLONS. PHOTOGRAPH
BY WILLIAM MCGUFFIN. COURTESY OF THE HARRISONBURG-ROCKINGHAM
HISTORICAL SOCIETY, DAYTON, VIRGINIA.

FIG. 8. EXAMPLES OF EMANUEL SUTER'S DECORATED STONEWARE JAR AND CROCK
FORMS. PHOTOGRAPH BY WILLIAM MCGUFFIN. COURTESY OF THE HARRISONBURG-
ROCKINGHAM HISTORICAL SOCIETY, DAYTON, VIRGINIA.

Harrisonburg, Va., _____ *188*

Mr _____

BOUGHT OF **E. SUTER & SON,**

Manufacturers of

ALL KINDS OF EARTHENWARE,

NEAR HARRISONBURG, VIRGINIA.

REGISTER JOB PRINT. HARRISONBURG, VA.

FIG. 9. BILLHEAD FOR E. SUTER & SON, C. 1885. PRIVATE COLLECTION.

FIG. 10. EXAMPLES OF EMANUEL SUTER'S EARTHENWARE STORAGE JARS. THE
MIDDLE EXAMPLE IS ATTRIBUTED TO ISAAC GOOD. PHOTOGRAPH BY WILLIAM
MCGUFFIN. COURTESY OF THE HARRISONBURG-ROCKINGHAM HISTORICAL
SOCIETY, DAYTON, VIRGINIA.

FIG. II. EXAMPLES OF EMANUEL SUTER'S STONEWARE CROCK FORMS.
PHOTOGRAPH BY WILLIAM MCGUFFIN. COURTESY OF THE HARRISONBURG-
ROCKINGHAM HISTORICAL SOCIETY, DAYTON, VIRGINIA.

FIG. 12. DRAIN TILE PRODUCED BY EMANUEL SUTER'S NEW ERECTION POTTERY.
PHOTOGRAPH BY WILLIAM MCGUFFIN. AUTHOR'S COLLECTION.

FIG. 13. DRAIN TILE
PRODUCED BY EMANUEL
SUTER'S NEW ERECTION
POTTERY. PHOTOGRAPH
BY WILLIAM MCGUFFIN.
AUTHOR'S COLLECTION.

FIG. 14. AN EXAMPLE OF AN EARTHEN-
WARE STOVE FLUE PRODUCED BY
EMANUEL SUTER'S NEW ERECTION
POTTERY. PHOTOGRAPH BY WILLIAM
MCGUFFIN. COURTESY OF THE
HARRISONBURG-ROCKINGHAM
HISTORICAL SOCIETY, DAYTON,
VIRGINIA.

FIG. 15. AN ARRAY OF FLOWER POTS AND A SAUCER PRODUCED BY EMANUEL SUTER'S
NEW ERECTION POTTERY. PHOTOGRAPH BY WILLIAM MCGUFFIN. COURTESY OF THE
HARRISONBURG-ROCKINGHAM HISTORICAL SOCIETY, DAYTON, VIRGINIA.

FIG. 16. TWO EXAMPLES (CENTER AND RIGHT) OF FORMALLY DECORATIVE VASES
AND A FOOTED FLOWER POT (LEFT) PRODUCED BY EMANUEL SUTER'S NEW ERECTION
POTTERY. THE CENTER EXAMPLE FEATURES MOLDED HANDLES. PHOTOGRAPH BY
WILLIAM MCGUFFIN. COURTESY OF THE HARRISONBURG-ROCKINGHAM HISTORICAL
SOCIETY, DAYTON, VIRGINIA.

FIG. 17. THE MOLDED FLOWER POT AND MARBLE BASE THAT
EMANUEL SUTER RECORDED MAKING IN 1887. PHOTOGRAPH
BY WILLIAM MCGUFFIN. COURTESY OF THE HARRISONBURG-
ROCKINGHAM HISTORICAL SOCIETY, DAYTON, VIRGINIA.

FIG. 18. TWO EXAMPLES OF EMANUEL SUTER'S CHICKEN DECORATION ON A STONEWARE
CHURN AND TWO-GALLON CROCK. PHOTOGRAPH BY WILLIAM MCGUFFIN. COURTESY OF
THE HARRISONBURG-ROCKINGHAM HISTORICAL SOCIETY, DAYTON, VIRGINIA.

FIG. 19. DRAIN TILE
SHERDS EXHIBITING
EXTRUSION MARKS FROM
THE PRESS AT EMANUEL
SUTER'S NEW ERECTION
POTTERY. PHOTOGRAPH
BY WILLIAM MCGUFFIN.
AUTHOR'S COLLECTION.

FIG. 21. EMANUEL AND ELIZABETH SUTER FAMILY PORTRAIT, TAKEN AUGUST 1, 1895,
BY HARRISONBURG PHOTOGRAPHER WILLIAM DEAN. STANDING LEFT TO RIGHT: JOHN
ROBERT SUTER, DAVID IRENAEUS SUTER, EMANUEL JACOB SUTER, EUGENE CLIFFORD
SUTER, PERRY GABRIEL SUTER, LAURA ELIZABETH SUTER WENGER. SEATED LEFT TO
RIGHT: CHRISTIAN CHARLES SUTER, SUSANNA VIRGINIA SUTER WENGER, EMANUEL
SUTER, ELIZABETH SWOPE SUTER, LILLIE HARRIET SUTER SHOWALTER, REUBEN
DANIEL SUTER, PETER SWOPE SUTER. AUTHOR'S COLLECTION.

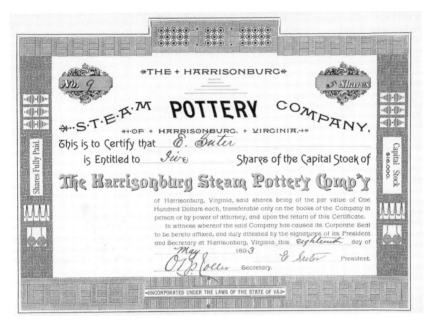

FIG. 22. STOCK CERTIFICATE FROM THE HARRISONBURG STEAM POTTERY COMPANY.
COURTESY OF THE VIRGINIA MENNONITE CONFERENCE ARCHIVE.

FIG. 23. THE VIRGINIA POTTERY, HARRISONBURG, VIRGINIA, 1890. THIS
IS A HAND-TINTED VERSION OF A BLACK-AND-WHITE ORIGINAL IMAGE.
COURTESY OF THE JULIUS F. RITCHIE COLLECTION.

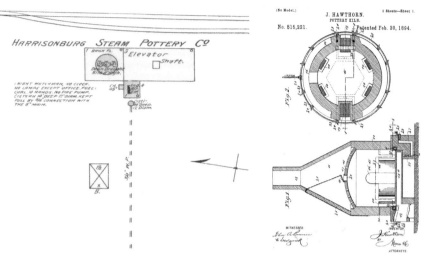

FIG. 24. DETAIL OF SANBORN MAP,
HARRISONBURG, VIRGINIA, 1897, SHOWING
THE HARRISONBURG STEAM POTTERY
COMPANY.

FIG. 25. JOHN HAWTHORN'S PATENT
FOR A POTTERY KILN, 1894.

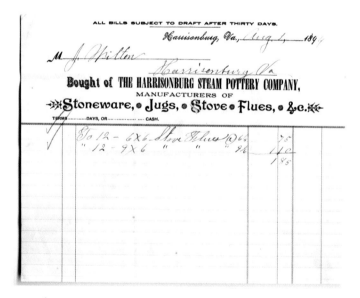

FIG. 26. BILL ISSUED BY HARRISONBURG STEAM POTTERY COMPANY,
DATED AUGUST 1, 1894. PRIVATE COLLECTION.

FIG. 27. THREE EXAMPLES OF WARE ATTRIBUTED TO THE HARRISONBURG
STEAM POTTERY COMPANY. ALL HAVE BELONGED TO SUTER FAMILY
MEMBERS SINCE THE PIECES WERE MANUFACTURED. PHOTOGRAPH BY
WILLIAM MCGUFFIN. AUTHOR'S COLLECTION.

FIG. 28. THREE EXAMPLES OF WARE ATTRIBUTED TO THE HARRISONBURG
STEAM POTTERY COMPANY. PHOTOGRAPH BY WILLIAM MCGUFFIN.
AUTHOR'S COLLECTION.

FIG. 29.TWO EXAMPLES OF JUGS ATTRIBUTED TO THE HARRISONBURG
STEAM POTTERY COMPANY. PHOTOGRAPH BY WILLIAM MCGUFFIN.
AUTHOR'S COLLECTION.

FREDERICK H. COWDEN LETTERS TO EMANUEL SUTER

The Emanuel Suter Collection, Virginia Mennonite Conference Archives, Eastern Mennonite University, Harrisonburg, Virginia, contains the following nine missives from Frederick H. Cowden to Emanuel Suter written during the period of 1887 to 1895. The letters reveal Emanuel Suter's continued interest in learning how other pottery manufacturers managed their businesses. Additionally, the letters demonstrate aspects of Cowden's own works in Harrisburg, Pennsylvania.

Harrisburg, Pa., Mar 4, 1887

Mr. E. Sutter [*sic*]

Dr Sir,

Mr. Wilcox handed me your letter. He is not in the stoneware business. I buy Albany slip from Mr. V. B. Wagner, Albany, New York. I can furnish you. Ship at $2.50 a bbl on car here.

Yours truly,
F. H. Cowden

Harrisburg, Pa., April 21, 1887

Mssrs E. Suter & Son

I have shipped you a bbl of slip today. To mix it put some of the slip to soak in water for a few days. Then add more water and stir it up until it is about as thick as milk, or looks greasy on the top. Trusting you will be successful in your experiment, I am

Yours truly,
F. H. Cowden

Harrisburg, Pa., Sept. 6, 1890

Mssrs E. Suter & Son

Gentlemen,

I received your letter of Aug. 25 and have been expecting the arrival of Mr. Suter Jr. He has not made his appearance yet, but I will be glad to welcome him whenever he can make it convenient to visit Harrisburg. I showed Mr. Reed (the man who built my kiln) your letters, he expected to wait and see your son. He could hardly give you an estimate [until] he knew definitely what size kiln &c you wanted. I think Mr. E. S. Thomas would do you as a turner, he can make large ware. He has been working at the stoneware business nearly all his life, although it is nearly 20 years since he worked in Hburg [Harrisburg]. I cannot say what he knows about setting and burning. He claims to know all about it. My shop will be closed a couple of months after the 1st of January and some of the men might go down there and start you up in good shape.

A kiln about 29 feet long and 14 feet wide outside will hold 4000 gal. setting as loose as I do. I saw a kiln about the size of mine in Lyons, New York the other week and the owner of the pottery say it will hold 10,000 gal. It was 19 ft. in diameter, a round kiln. I can let you have those molds whenever you need them.

Yours truly,

   F. H. Cowden

Harrisburg, Pa., Sept. 29, 1890

Mssrs. E. Suter & Son,

I have been very busy since receiving your letter and should have answered sooner. Some of the questions you ask were answered in my letter which passed yours on the way. I require my turners to have enough ware ready for the kiln when we are ready to set it so as not to delay the setting. I pay about 1 1/2 cats. per gal. for turning although that is more than most potteries pay, however, I require good work and have good turners.

I mix 25 to 50 per cent of Woodbridge clay with Amboy. You can use as much as you please. Woodbridge clay spoils to the outside color of the ware more than Amboy, but is much safer to burn and cool. The kiln you saw us burn off was all right except that the ware was a little brown. I have no trouble except that with any kiln. If you want the molds I can send them to you at any time. If you are going to run a jigger wheel they will be cheaper than to make them. Any further information I can give you will be gladly furnished, and come on and see us whenever you can. Have had a big rush for ware the past three weeks and run down stock considerable.

Your Friend,

F. H. Cowden

Harrisburg, Pa., April 8, 1891

Mr. E. Suter

Dear Sir,
I hardly know what to advise you in regard to using Rose and Sons clay but think it would be safer to use Ernst and Furmans mixed with Woodbridge to start with. You have a new enterprise and should take no more risks than is absolutely necessary at the start. How would it be to get a car of both the Furman and the Rose clay and mix each separate with Woodbridge using only enough Rose clay to give it a good trial the first kiln, and if it served the purpose you could keep on using it. Perhaps Rose and son would refer you to parties who are using his clay who could give you all the information you wanted. We are burning off kiln this morning and I must go and see how they are getting on out at the kiln. Write soon.

Your Friend,

F. H. Cowden

Harrisburg, Pa., June 26, 1891

Mr. E. Suter

Dear Sir,

I will come down to your place and direct the burning of your kiln on the following terms viz. You to have good Bituminous coal and supply the men to do the burning. And you to pay my railroad fare and expenses to and from Harrisonburg and Lodge me while there.

And if I make a successful burn pay me $20. I cannot come next week but can start Monday July 6. It is not necessary for me to see the floor of your kiln, only leave room for a few stands at the door and do not close up the door until I come. I suppose I can crawl under kiln and see how flues are arranged there. I will come on these conditions but recollect it is necessary to have good coal without much slack in it to get up heat. But I think I can do it if it is in the coal to do it. Awaiting your reply I remain

Yours truly,

    F. H. Cowden

Harrisburg, Pa., June 30, 1891

Mr. E. Suter

Dear Sir,

It will be impossible for me to be in Harrisonburg by Wednesday now as we are very busy here and have made no arrangements about going. Possibly you will be more fortunate with your kiln this time.

Very respectfully,

    F. H. Cowden

Harrisburg, Pa., July 3, 1891

Mr. E. Suter

Dear Sir,

I would only close the damper about 8 or 12 inches of the trench opening when salting. If you have trouble getting up heat this time do as follows. Put fire brick up at side of iron doors and keep the cold air from passing over fire. Always recollect *that cold air over fire checks heat*. Break up coal after and keep a good draft below under the fire.

Yours truly,

    F. H. Cowden

Harrisburg Pa., March 23, 1895

E. Suter Esq.
Harrisonburg, VA

Dear Sir,

To make the circular fire brick you inquire about we have rings made of galvanized iron of the required dimensions allowing for shrinkage and send them to any fire brick works and have them make them. We send ours to R. B. Winton and Sons Phillipsburg Pa., but you can probably have them made nearer home as well. We are very glad to hear from you again and are all quite well.

Yours very truly,

F. H. Cowden

NOTES

Introduction

1. Emanuel Suter Diary, 1 January 1893, Emanuel Suter Collection, Virginia Mennonite Conference Archives, Eastern Mennonite Univ., Harrisonburg, VA.
2. Ibid., 19 April 1897.
3. Wayne Franklin, *A Rural Carpenter's World: The Craft in a Nineteenth-Century New York Township* (Iowa City: Univ. of Iowa Press, 1990), 5.
4. L. Diane Barnes, Brian Schoen, and Frank Towers, eds., *The Old South's Modern Worlds: Slavery, Region, and Nation in the Age of Progress* (New York: Oxford Univ. Press, 2011), 4.

Chapter 1

1. For a concise description of the importance of the Shenandoah Valley in the Civil War see James M. McPherson, *Ordeal By Fire: The Civil War and Reconstruction* (New York: Alfred A. Knopf, 1982), 184, 239–42. McPherson notes that the Valley "formed a natural route of invasion, but this favored the Confederacy rather than the Union because it ran southwest, away from Richmond and the main battle theater in Virginia. Indeed the Confederacy used the valley three times for invasions or threats against the North . . . for in that direction the valley pointed toward important Northern cities, including Washington itself" (184). See also John W. Wayland, *Twenty-five Chapters on the Shenandoah Valley, To Which is Appended a Concise History of the Civil War in the Valley*, 2nd ed. (Harrisonburg, VA: C. J. Carrier Company, 1976).
2. For an account of Sheridan's actions in the Shenandoah Valley see John L. Heatwole, *The Burning: Sheridan's Devastation of the Shenandoah Valley* (Berryville, VA: Rockbridge Publishing, 1998).
3. Quoted in David S. Rodes and Norman R. Wenger, *Unionists and the Civil War Experience in the Shenandoah Valley*, ed. Emmert F. Bittinger, vol. 3 (Dayton, VA: Valley Research Associates and Valley Brethren-Mennonite Heritage Center, 2005), 743. Southern Claims Commission, Claim 8336, 21 April 1871.
4. Emanuel Suter, "A Letter from Harrisburg, Pa.," *Herald of Truth* 2, no. 4 (1865): 29.
5. Several scholarly works look at this movement of refugees out of the Shenandoah Valley. James O. Lehman and Steven M. Nolt devote a chapter to this period in *Mennonites,*

Amish, and the American Civil War (Baltimore: Johns Hopkins Univ. Press, 2007). Harry Anthony Brunk provides a thorough examination of the importance of this journey to Shenandoah Valley Mennonites in his *History of Mennonites in Virginia, 1727–1900* (Harrisonburg, VA: by the author, 1959), 167–72. See also Samuel Horst, *Mennonites in the Confederacy: A Study in Civil War Pacifism* (Scottdale, PA: Herald Press, 1967), 96–110.

6. For studies of cultural life in the Valley see Scott Hamilton Suter, *Shenandoah Valley Folklife* (Jackson: Univ. Press of Mississippi, 1999), Elmer Lewis Smith, John G. Stewart, and M. Ellsworth Kyger, *The Pennsylvania Germans of the Shenandoah Valley* (Allentown, PA: Schleter's, 1964), Klaus Wust, *The Virginia Germans* (Charlottesville: Univ. of Virginia Press, 1969), and Kenneth E. Koons and Warren R. Hofstra, *After the Backcountry: Rural Life in the Great Valley of Virginia, 1800–1900* (Knoxville: Univ. of Tennessee Press, 2000).

7. D. W. Meinig has asserted that by the middle of the eighteenth century "in the larger patterns of culture and circulation Greater Pennsylvania had cast a long thin line across the whole breadth of the western frontier of Greater Virginia" (160). See *The Shaping of American: A Geographical Perspective on 500 Years of History*, vol. 1, *Atlantic America, 1492–1800* (New Haven: Yale Univ. Press, 1986), 153–60.

8. Since the Shenandoah River flows northeast, the phrase "down the Valley" refers to a northerly direction. See Warren R. Hofstra and Karl Raitz, eds., *The Great Valley Road of Virginia: Shenandoah Landscapes from Prehistory to the Present* (Charlottesville: Univ. of Virginia Press, 2010).

9. For an excellent example of cultural geography applied to a pottery tradition see John Winberry, "The Cultural Hearth of the Southern Pottery Tradition: The Historical Geographic Framework," in *Crossroads of Clay: The Southern Alkaline-Glazed Stoneware Tradition*, ed. Catherine Wilson Horne (Columbia: McKissick Museum, The Univ. of South Carolina, 1990), 5–15.

10. H. E. Comstock provides a thorough description of Shenandoah Valley clay in *The Pottery of the Shenandoah Valley Region* (Winston-Salem, NC: The Museum of Early Southern Decorative Arts, 1994), 21–25.

11. See Robert D. Mitchell, *Commercialization on the Frontier: Perspectives on the Early Shenandoah Valley* (Charlottesville: Univ. Press of Virginia, 1977), 8.

12. For histories and descriptions of the Shenandoah Valley see Mitchell, *Commercialization*, 19–25; Samuel Kercheval, *A History of the Valley of Virginia*, 7th ed. (Harrisonburg, VA: C. J. Carrier Co., 1986); William Couper, *History of the Shenandoah Valley*, 3 vols. (New York: Lewis Historical Publishing Co., 1952); and Wayland, *Twenty-five Chapters*. Detailed studies of the region can be found in Kenneth E. Koons and Warren R. Hofstra, eds., *After the Backcountry: Rural Life in the Great Valley of Virginia, 1800–1900* (Knoxville: Univ. of Tennessee Press, 2000) and Warren R. Hofstra and Karl Raitz, eds., *The Great Valley Road of Virginia: Shenandoah Landscapes from Prehistory to the Present* (Charlottesville: Univ. of Virginia Press, 2010).

13. Mitchell, *Commercialization*, 16–19. Also see Warren R. Hofstra, *The Planting of New Virginia: Settlement and Landscape in the Shenandoah Valley*, (Baltimore: Johns Hopkins Univ. Press, 2005).

14. See Smith et al., *The Pennsylvania Germans*; Wust, *The Virginia Germans*; John Stewart and Elmer Smith, "The Survival of German Dialects & Customs in the Shenandoah Valley," *Society for the History of the Germans in Maryland*, Report 31 (1963): 66–70; Edward A. Chappell, "Cultural Change in the Shenandoah Valley: Northern Augusta County Houses before 1861," (Master's thesis, Univ. of Virginia, 1977).

15. For instance, Mitchell notes in *Commercialization* that a Staunton merchant William Crow made regular cattle drives down the Shenandoah Valley and on to Philadelphia in the 1750s and 1760s (148–49).

16. Mitchell, *Commercialization*, 189–90.

17. Mitchell, *Commercialization*, 240.

18. See Mary Eugenia Suter, *Memories of Yesteryear* (Waynesboro, VA: Charles F. McClung, 1959), 1–4, and Marian B. Suter, ed., *More Memories of Yesteryear: An Updated Genealogy of the Family of Daniel Suter (1808–1873)* (Harrisonburg, VA: Campbell, 2017).

19. See Joseph W. Glass, *The Pennsylvania Culture Region: A View from the Barn* (Ann Arbor: UMI Research Press, 1986); Amos Long, Jr., *The Pennsylvania German Family Farm* (Breinigsville, PA: The Pennsylvania German Society, 1972), 315; Robert F. Ensminger, *The Pennsylvania Barn: Its Origin, Evolution, and Distribution in North America* (Baltimore: Johns Hopkins Univ. Press, 1992), 147–53.

20. Numerous letters written to Emanuel Suter in German can be found in the Suter collections.

21. Emanuel Suter's father, Daniel, of Swiss origin but having emigrated from France in 1820, spoke French, German, and English, as well as Swiss and Welsh dialects; his story was not uncommon. Suter, *Memories*, 4.

22. Interviews with Alice Heatwole Suter and Grace Suter Grove, both from Rockingham County, confirm that a form of German known in the Valley as "Dutch" was understood by their parents, although not spoken by them (Interviews by author, 3 August 1992). Orpha Horst, a member of the Old Order Mennonite community near Dayton, Virginia, stated that her father spoke "Dutch" as well as English as late as 1990 (Interview by author, 7 June 1990). The most comprehensive study of the Pennsylvania German language is Mark L. Louden, "The Pennsylvania German Language" in Simon J. Bronner and Joshua R. Brown, eds., *Pennsylvania Germans: An Interpretive Encyclopedia* (Baltimore: Johns Hopkins Univ. Press, 2017), 79–107. Another more specific and useful essay also in Bronner and Brown is Donald B. Kraybill, Steven M. Nolt, and Edsel Burdge, Jr., "Language Use among Anabaptist Groups," 108–30.

23. Henry Glassie, *Pattern in the Material Folk Culture of the Eastern United States* (Philadelphia: Univ. of Pennsylvania Press, 1968), 38–39; Hans Kurath, *A Word Geography of the Eastern United States* (Ann Arbor: Univ. of Michigan Press, 1949); see also Craig M. Carver, *American Regional Dialects: A Word Geography* (Ann Arbor: Univ. of Michigan Press, 1987), 161–203.

24. Kurath, *A Word Geography of the Eastern United States*, 30.

25. Ibid., 35.

26. Given that many residents were bilingual, Klaus Wust has suggested in *The Virginia Germans* that political candidates in the Valley were at a considerable disadvantage if they

were monolingual, noting that "until about 1840, a command of the German language was patently an asset for a political candidate in large portions of the Shenandoah Valley" (117–18).

27. See Wust; Carl F. Bowman, *Brethren Society: The Cultural Transformation of a "Peculiar People"* (Baltimore: Johns Hopkins Univ. Press, 1995); Richard K. MacMaster, *Land, Piety, Peoplehood: The Establishment of Mennonite Communities in America, 1683–1790* (Scottdale, PA: Herald Press, 1985); Roger E. Sappington, *The Brethren in Virginia* (Harrisonburg, VA: Park View Press, 1973); J. C. Wenger, *The Mennonite Church in America* (Scottdale, PA: Herald Press, 1966); D. H. Zigler, *A History of the Brethren in Virginia* (Elgin: Brethren Publishing House, 1908); J. S. Hartzler and Daniel Kauffman, *Mennonite Church History* (Scottdale, PA: Mennonite Book and Tract Society, 1905).

28. Harold S. Bender, "The Choice of Pennsylvania" in Wenger, *The Mennonite Church in America*, 52–68; L. J. Heatwole, "The Virginia Conference," in Hartzler and Kauffman, *Mennonite Church History*, 198–224.

29. Wust, *The Virginia Germans*, 94–95.

30. For Brethren congregations see Zigler, following page 28; for all German congregations in Virginia in 1810 see Wust, 133.

31. See Harold S. Bender et al., eds., *The Mennonite Encyclopedia: A Comprehensive Reference Work on the Anabaptist-Mennonite Movement* (Scottdale, PA: Mennonite Publishing House, 1959), s.v. "Rockingham County." The location of Eastern Mennonite University and Seminary in Harrisonburg, Virginia (since 1917), the county seat of Rockingham County, and Bridgewater College (affiliated with the Church of the Brethren) also attests to the importance of the area to the Anabaptist community of the eastern United States.

32. Hofstra and Raitz, *The Great Valley Road of Virginia: Shenandoah Landscapes*, 10.

33. Ibid., 11.

34. Emanuel Suter to Daniel Suter, June 17, 1865, Emanuel Suter Collection, Virginia Mennonite Conference Archives, Eastern Mennonite Univ., Harrisonburg, VA.

35. Glass, *The Pennsylvania Culture Region*, 21.

36. Wilbur Zelinsky, "The Changing Character of North American Culture Areas," in *Regional Studies: The Interplay of Land and People*, ed. Glen Lich (College Station: Texas A & M Univ. Press, 1992), 125.

37. Michael Conzen, "Ethnicity on the Land," in *The Making of the American Landscape*, ed. Michael Conzen (London: HarperCollins Academic, 1990), 241–42.

38. D. W. Meinig, *The Shaping of America: A Geographical Perspective on 500 Years of History*, vol. 2, *Continental America, 1800–1867* (New Haven: Yale Univ. Press, 1995), 389.

39. For other specific examples see Scott Hamilton Suter, *Tradition and Fashion* (Dayton, VA: Harrisonburg-Rockingham Historical Society, 1996) and Jeffrey S. Evans, *Come In and Have a Seat* (Winchester, VA: Museum of the Shenandoah Valley, 2010).

40. Meinig, *The Shaping of America*, vol. 2, *Continental America, 1800–1867*, 389.

41. Ibid., 390.

42. John Majewski, *A House Dividing: Economic Development in Pennsylvania and Virginia before the Civil War* (New York: Cambridge Univ. Press, 2000), 11.

43. Suter, *Shenandoah Valley Folklife*, xii.

Chapter 2

1. Daniel Suter's birth was recorded in *Etat Civil Commune de Lepuix (Delle)* which can be accessed at http://www.archives.territoiredebelfort.fr/ark:/12997/a011341578574xgx DYI/1/1. Tom and Marcia Suter translated this document from the original French.

2. For a history of the Heatwole family in Virginia see Harry Anthony Brunk, *David Heatwole and His Descendants* (Harrisonburg, VA: Park View Press, 1987).

3. Emanuel Suter Diary, 28 March 1896, Emanuel Suter Collection, Virginia Mennonite Conference Archives, Eastern Mennonite Univ., Harrisonburg, VA.

4. Rockingham County (VA) Chancery Causes, 1781–1946, Shem Heatwole vs. Jonathan Clary's Adm., 1858–021, Local Government Records Collection, Rockingham Court Records, Library of Virginia, Richmond, VA.

5. David S. Rodes and Norman R. Wenger, *Unionists and the Civil War Experience in the Shenandoah Valley*, ed. Emmert F. Bittinger, vol. 3 (Dayton, VA: Valley Research Associates, 2005), 741.

6. L. J. Heatwole, "Sketch of the Life and Work of Emanuel Suter," in *Mennonite Year-Book and Directory* (Scottdale, PA: Mennonite Board of Charitable Homes and Missions, 1906), 31–33.

7. H. E. Comstock, *The Pottery of the Shenandoah Valley Region* (Winston-Salem, NC: The Museum of Early Southern Decorative Arts, 1994), 386–87. Jeffrey S. Evans and Scott Hamilton Suter discuss Coffman's stylistic influence on Rockingham County pottery in *"A Great Deal of Stone & Earthenware": The Rockingham County, Virginia School of Folk Pottery* (Dayton, VA: Harrisonburg-Rockingham Historical Society, 2004), 5–9.

8. Andrew Coffman died in 1853. Reuben S. Coffman appears in 1860 census as a potter residing with John D. Heatwole. See Comstock, *The Pottery of the Shenandoah Valley Region*, 386–89.

9. Tax Receipt and Note, Emanuel Suter Collection, Virginia Mennonite Conference Archives, Eastern Mennonite Univ., Harrisonburg, VA.

10. Suter, *Memories of Yesteryear*, 7.

11. Emanuel's son Peter (Swope) began working full-time as a cabinetmaker in the late 1890s and originally built a shop on the Suter homestead. Adding more advanced tools to the hand tools of his grandfather, he expanded his business and moved to various sites and eventually opened Suter's Craft Shop in Harrisonburg, Virginia, in 1952. Swope's son Owen continued the business upon his father's death, and eventually other family members maintained the business (Suter, *Memories of Yesteryear*, 101–03). Suter's Craft Shop produced furniture in Harrisonburg into the twenty-first century.

12. The origins of this community name lie in the background of an early Presbyterian minister in Rockingham County, Virginia. Alexander Miller, who was ordained by the Presbytery of Letterkenny at the New Erection in County Tyrone, Ireland, in 1745,

immigrated to America and became the pastor at both Cooks Creek and Peaked Mountain churches in the county. The Cooks Creek church building, located near the present town of Dayton, was torn down in 1780, and the congregation moved to a new location. The second church building at this location was built in 1834 and named "New Erection" in honor of the influential pastor's ordination site in Ireland. The community around the church has maintained the name, although the church has become known once again by original name, Cooks Creek Presbyterian Church. See Milo Custer, *The Reverend Alexander Miller of Virginia and Some of His Descendants* (Bloomington, IL: s.n., 1910).

13. See Evans and Suter, *"A Great Deal of Stone and Earthenware,"* 12, plates 23–24.

14. Rodes and Wenger, *Unionists and the Civil War Experience in the Shenandoah Valley*, 752–53. This is contrary to previous explanations that Suter was relieved from military service so that he could make ware for the Confederacy, a claim that is further disproved by the fact that Suter furnished a substitute and then paid the $500 fee which released his substitute from military service. See Rodes and Wenger, 742.

15. Hand-written note, Emanuel Suter Collection, Virginia Mennonite Conference Archives, Eastern Mennonite Univ., Harrisonburg, VA.

16. Suter, *Memories of Yesteryear*, 33.

17. Harry Brunk covers this topic in detail in *David Heatwole and His Descendants*. See pages 157–77.

18. Suter's diary describes in detail the trip from Harrisonburg into Pennsylvania and the time that the family spent there. The family left their home on October 5, 1864, and returned on June 10, 1865. Emanuel Suter Diary, 1864 and 1865, Emanuel Suter Collection, Virginia Mennonite Conference Archives, Eastern Mennonite Univ., Harrisonburg, VA.

19. Emanuel Suter Diary, 13 August 1866, Emanuel Suter Collection, Virginia Mennonite Conference Archives, Eastern Mennonite Univ., Harrisonburg, VA.

20. Ibid., 18 September 1866. Samuel Shrum was a mason and brick manufacturer from nearby Dayton, VA.

21. Emanuel Suter's obituary reported that as "a citizen he embodied that highest of all virtues—the sinking of self-interest for the common welfare." *Rockingham Register* (Harrisonburg, VA), December 19, 1902.

22. Theron Schlabach, *Peace, Faith, Nation: Mennonites and Amish in Nineteenth-Century America* (Scottdale, PA: Herald Press, 1985), 118.

23. Suter concluded every diary entry with a religious thought such as: "It is ever good to thank & praise our dear Heavenly Father for his tender love & mercy." Emanuel Suter Diary, December 14, 1893, Emanuel Suter Collection, Virginia Mennonite Conference Archives, Eastern Mennonite Univ., Harrisonburg, VA.

24. Suter declared to the Southern Claims Commission: "I furnished a substitute for the Confederate Army to keep from going into the army myself. My substitute was soon released upon my paying my fine of $500." Rodes and Wenger, *Unionists and the Civil War*, 742.

25. Although the Virginia government did allow pacifist groups such as the Quakers, Brethren, and Mennonites to pay a fee for exemption from military service or furnish a substitute,

many followers of these faiths were not members of their given church. It is customary that baptism into the Mennonite Church does not take place until the believer is twenty-five years old. Because of this many Mennonite men under that age were conscripted despite the fact that they did profess the Mennonite faith. Such forced involvement led to many desertions and refusals to serve. See Schlabach, *Peace, Faith, Nation*, 173–200; Horst, *Mennonites in the Confederacy*, 28–95. Horst discusses Emanuel Suter's involvement on page 87.

26. See Brunk, *History of Mennonites in Virginia, 1727–1900*, 228–35.

27. *Minutes of the Virginia Mennonite Conference*, 2nd ed. (Scottdale, PA: Mennonite Publishing House, 1950), xxiii.

28. L. J. Heatwole, "Suter," *Herald of Truth* (January 1903): 7.

29. Harold S. Bender, C. Henry Smithe, et al., *The Mennonite Encyclopedia* (Scottdale, PA: The Mennonite Publishing House, 1955), s.v. "Lot," by H. S. Bender.

30. Jacob Hildebrand, Waynesboro, VA, to Emanuel Suter, March 27, 1879, Emanuel Suter Collection, Virginia Mennonite Conference Archives, Eastern Mennonite Univ., Harrisonburg, VA.

31. Lewis J. Heatwole, Dale Enterprise, VA, to Emanuel Suter, 27 March, 1880, Emanuel Suter Collection, Virginia Mennonite Conference Archives, Eastern Mennonite Univ., Harrisonburg, VA.

32. Ibid.

33. *The Minutes of the Virginia Mennonite Conference* (37) record the following: "The Petition to Conference; ORDINATION—Numerously signed by members of the church asking that the plan for choosing candidates for official positions in the church be brought more in line with the Confession of Faith and scriptural qualifications, was read and commented on during entire afternoon session, and on being renewed the following morning was, finally dismissed."

34. See Brunk, *History of Mennonites in Virginia, 1727–1900*, 196–97, 199–227. See also Schlabach, *Peace, Faith, Nation*, 226–29.

35. Schlabach, *Peace, Faith, Nation*, 228.

36. Brunk, *David Heatwole and His Descendants*, 205–6. See also E. Richard Good, *Enlarging the Borders: Virginia Mennonite Conference, 150 Years of Expansion* (Harrisonburg: Virginia Mennonite Conference, 1985), 45.

37. Brunk, *History of Mennonites in Virginia, 1727–1900*, 222.

38. Ibid., 351.

39. Ibid., 221.

40. *Report of the Commissioner of Agriculture for 1874*, "Modern Farming in America," Augustin L. Taveau (Washington, DC: Government Printing Office, 1875), 280. Suter may or may not have read this report; however, he did request information from the Department of Agriculture. A letter written to the Honorable John T. Harris, House of Representatives, from the Commissioner of Agriculture regarding Suter's inquiry about reports indicates that he did view such tracts as a source of information. Commissioner Wm. LeDue to Honorable Jn. T. Harris, Washington, DC, June 4, 1879, Emanuel Suter

Collection, Virginia Mennonite Conference Archives, Eastern Mennonite Univ., Harrisonburg, VA.

41. Edward L. Ayers, *The Promise of the New South: Life After Reconstruction* (New York: Oxford Univ. Press, 1992), 190–91.

42. Kenneth E. Koons, "'The Staple of Our Country': Wheat in the Regional Farm Economy of the Nineteenth-Century Valley of Virginia," in *After the Backcountry: Rural Life in the Great Valley of Virginia, 1800–1900* (Knoxville: Univ. of Tennessee Press, 2000), 6. Koons' essay is the most comprehensive study of wheat production and other crops in the nineteenth-century Shenandoah Valley.

43. Koons, "'The Staple of Our Country,'" 4.

44. Suter, Memories of *Yesteryear*, 76.

45. Wayne D. Rasmussen points out that these changes took place primarily in the northern United States, noting that the "South did not contribute to increased agricultural productivity during this period." "The Civil War: A Catalyst of Agricultural Revolution," *Agricultural History* 39 (October 1965): 188.

46. Writing to his friend Emanuel Suter while visiting Masontown, Pennsylvania in 1883, Rockingham County native C. H. Brunk bragged that "there is more attention paid to grazing than agriculture here—We can beat them raising wheat by one-half." C. H. Brunk to Emanuel Suter, May 5, 1883, Emanuel Suter Collection, Virginia Mennonite Conference Archives, Eastern Mennonite Univ., Harrisonburg, VA. Brunk's pride in the Valley's wheat production indicates the importance of that crop in the area.

47. For an in depth study of flailing and the importance of threshing in Pennsylvania see Beauveau Borie, IV, *Farming and Folk Society: Threshing Among the Pennsylvania Germans* (Ann Arbor: UMI Research Press, 1986). For a description of flails see pages 6–11.

48. John T. Schlebecker, *Whereby We Thrive: A History of American Farming, 1607–1972* (Ames: Iowa State Univ. Press, 1975), 188–220.

49. Emanuel Suter Diary, 15 July 1872, Emanuel Suter Collection, Virginia Mennonite Conference Archives, Eastern Mennonite Univ., Harrisonburg, VA. Papers within the Suter collection suggest that Jacob may have been the primary owner of the threshing machine and that Emanuel came into the arrangement after Jacob. The census for 1870 lists Jacob D. Suter as "Manager Thresh Machine."

50. Ibid., July 29, 1872. Suter always capitalized the word "machine," perhaps signaling its importance to his way of thinking.

51. Ibid., 3 September 1867.

52. Garver & Flanagan to Emanuel Suter, 6 March 1873, Emanuel Suter Collection, Virginia Mennonite Conference Archives, Eastern Mennonite Univ., Harrisonburg, VA.

53. Emanuel Suter Diary, 9–14 July 1875, Emanuel Suter Collection, Virginia Mennonite Conference Archives, Eastern Mennonite Univ., Harrisonburg, VA.

54. Ibid., 15 July 1875.

55. Ibid., 16 July 1875.

56. Emanuel Suter, Harrisonburg, VA, to Peter Shoemaker, July 1878, Schumacher Manuscripts, Musselman Library, Bluffton Univ., Bluffton, OH.

57. Wayne D. Rasmussen, "The Impact of Technological Change on American Agriculture, 1862–1962," *Journal of Economic History* 20 (December 1962): 580. For histories of the reaper and its importance to farmers see Cyrus McCormick, *The Century of the Reaper* (Boston: Houghton, Mifflin Co., 1931) and Merritt Finley Miller, *The Evolution of Reaping Machines*, United States Department of Agriculture, Farmers' Bulletin No. 103 (Washington, DC: Government Printing Office, 1902).

58. David B. Danbom, *Born in the Country: A History of Rural America* (Baltimore: Johns Hopkins Univ. Press, 1995): 111.

59. Emanuel Suter Diary, 3 June 1870, Emanuel Suter Collection, Virginia Mennonite Conference Archives, Eastern Mennonite Univ., Harrisonburg, VA.

60. Ibid., 14 June 1870. Adam Showalter was the local representative of Marsh, Grier, & Co., manufacturers of the Valley Chief Self-raking Reaper and Mower. See Marsh, Grier, & Co., Mount Joy, Lancaster County, PA, to Emanuel Suter, 28 January 1871, Emanuel Suter Collection, Virginia Mennonite Conference Archives, Eastern Mennonite Univ., Harrisonburg, VA.

61. Ibid.

62. Marsh, Grier, & Co., Mount Joy, Lancaster County, PA, to Emanuel Suter, February 9, 1871, Emanuel Suter Collection, Virginia Mennonite Conference Archives, Eastern Mennonite Univ., Harrisonburg, VA. See also letter of March 24, 1871.

63. Marsh, Grier, & Co., Mount Joy, Lancaster County, PA, to Emanuel Suter, April 20, 1871, Emanuel Suter Collection, Virginia Mennonite Conference Archives, Eastern Mennonite Univ., Harrisonburg, VA.

64. Marsh, Grier, & Co., Mount Joy, Lancaster County, PA, to Emanuel Suter, May 6, 1871, Emanuel Suter Collection, Virginia Mennonite Conference Archives, Eastern Mennonite Univ., Harrisonburg, VA.

65. Emanuel Suter Diary, 18 May 1871, Emanuel Suter Collection, Virginia Mennonite Conference Archives, Eastern Mennonite Univ., Harrisonburg, VA.

66. All of the above references are from Emanuel Suter Diary for 1871, Emanuel Suter Collection, Virginia Mennonite Conference Archives, Eastern Mennonite Univ., Harrisonburg, VA.

67. John Grier wrote to Emanuel Suter about making arrangements with a Harrisonburg merchant: "Please write again to us & if you think they do not want the agency only to kill our machine & sell the others." Mount Joy, Lancaster County, PA, 5 March 1872, Emanuel Suter Collection, Virginia Mennonite Conference Archives, Eastern Mennonite Univ., Harrisonburg, VA.

68. Ibid.

69. Marsh and Comp, Mount Joy, PA, to Emanuel Suter, 8 March 1876, Emanuel Suter Collection, Virginia Mennonite Conference Archives, Eastern Mennonite Univ., Harrisonburg, VA. John A. Grier bought out the interests of his partners in 1872 and became the sole manufacturer of the Valley Chief Reaper and Mower. In 1876, he sold his interests to Charles C. Marsh and Alfred H. Comp.

70. Ibid.

71. E. S. Mitchell, Harrisonburg, VA, to Emanuel Suter, 17 June 1878, Emanuel Suter

Collection, Virginia Mennonite Conference Archives, Eastern Mennonite Univ., Harrisonburg, VA.

72. See Rasmussen, "The Civil War: A Catalyst of Agricultural Revolution" and Rasmussen, "The Impact of Technological Change on American Agriculture, 1862–1962."

73. Sally McMurry, *Families and Farmhouses in Nineteenth-Century America: Vernacular Design and Social Change* (Knoxville: Univ. of Tennessee Press, 1997), viii. Also see Sally McMurry, "Who Read the Agricultural Journals? Evidence from Chenango County, New York, 1839–1865," *Agricultural History* 63 (Fall 1989): 1–19.

74. Taveau, "Modern Farming in America," 281.

75. Robert W. Rydell, *All the World's a Fair: Visions of Empire at American International Expositions, 1876–1916* (Chicago: Univ. of Chicago Press, 1984), 11.

76. Quoted in John A. Kouwenhoven, *The Arts in Modern American Civilization* (New York: W. W. Norton, 1948), 25.

77. Emanuel Suter Diary, 26 October 1876, Emanuel Suter Collection, Virginia Mennonite Conference Archives, Eastern Mennonite Univ., Harrisonburg, VA. Suter's former business associate in reaper sales, John A. Grier, worked at the US Mint and had invited him to visit there if he attended the Centennial Exhibition. John A. Grier, Philadelphia, PA, 26 July 1876, to Emanuel Suter, Emanuel Suter Collection, Virginia Mennonite Conference Archives, Eastern Mennonite Univ., Harrisonburg, VA. Suter remarked in his letter home that he "saw John A. Grier, he showed me all around the concern. I saw [a] million dollars' worth of Gold and Silver." Emanuel Suter, Philadelphia, PA, October 1876, to Elizabeth Suter, Emanuel Suter Collection, Virginia Mennonite Conference Archives, Eastern Mennonite Univ., Harrisonburg, VA.

78. It is difficult to determine exactly what pottery enterprise Suter visited. In her checklist of Philadelphia potters, 1800–1850, Susan H. Myers does not identify a business by that name. *Handcraft to Industry: Philadelphia Ceramics in the First Half of the Nineteenth Century* (Washington, DC: Smithsonian Institution Press, 1980): 50–90. This, of course, may simply indicate that the pottery Suter mentions opened after 1850. Possibly, he is referring to the Philadelphia Terra Cotta Works, since he possessed an illustrated pamphlet from that business. The undated pamphlet shows designs for twelve different molded vases.

79. Emanuel Suter, Philadelphia, PA, October, 1876 to Elizabeth Suter, Emanuel Suter Collection, Virginia Mennonite Conference Archives, Eastern Mennonite Univ., Harrisonburg, VA.

80. James D. McCabe, *The Illustrated History of the Centennial Exhibition* (Philadelphia: The National Publishing Company, 1876), 124.

81. Emanuel Suter Diary, 19 October 1893, Emanuel Suter Collection, Virginia Mennonite Conference Archives, Eastern Mennonite Univ., Harrisonburg, VA.

82. Benjamin Truman, *History of the World's Fair Being a Complete and Authentic Description of the Columbian Exposition From its Inception* (Philadelphia: Syndicate Publishing, 1893), 313.

83. Ibid., 322.

84. Henry Adams, *The Education of Henry Adams* (Boston: Privately Printed, 1907; reprint, New York: Literary Classics of the United States), 1033.

85. Ibid., 1033.

86. Rydell, *All the World's a Fair*, 46.

87. The Rockingham County Fair continues to be held annually.

88. *Rockingham Register* (Harrisonburg, VA), May 27, 1893.

89. Ibid., 2 June 1893. Orra Langhorne, a columnist for the *Southern Workman*, reported her reactions to the first Spring Fair in Harrisonburg in August of 1892: "[At Harrisonburg an agricultural] fair was going on and the thriving little town, much grown and improved since my last visit, wore a holiday aspect. Assembly Park was given over for the day to a meeting of the Farmer's Alliance, which was out in force. . . . Machinery of many kinds, much of it in operation, was on exhibition. . . . A steam-mill was running, laundry and cooking establishments in full operation, tables filled with attractive viands were set—to which all were invited—while enough machines for all sorts of work were scattered about under the spreading trees to inspire the hope that all weary hands could rest and the owners bask in the knowledge that work was 'doing itself'." Quoted in Charles E. Wynes, ed., *Southern Sketches from Virginia, 1881–1901* (Charlottesville: Univ. of Virginia Press, 1964), 114–15.

90. Emanuel Suter Diary, 31 May 1893, Emanuel Suter Collection, Virginia Mennonite Conference Archives, Eastern Mennonite Univ., Harrisonburg, VA.

91. Suter noted in his diary that "Perry [a son] hauled the ware in from the fair ground we had out there on exhibition." 3 June 1893, Emanuel Suter Collection, Virginia Mennonite Conference Archives, Eastern Mennonite Univ., Harrisonburg, VA.

92. Richard L. Bushman, *The Refinement of America: Persons, Houses, Cities* (New York: Alfred A. Knopf, 1992), 259.

93. An 1879 fire insurance policy notes the size of the house and the addition: "Dwelling House 20' × 30', Ell 18' × 24.'" The West Rockingham Mutual Fire Insurance Co., Emanuel Suter Collection, Virginia Mennonite Conference Archives, Eastern Mennonite Univ., Harrisonburg, VA.

94. Bushman, *The Refinement of America*, 258.

95. Bushman, *The Refinement of America*, 251. See also McMurry, *Families and Farmhouses* for a discussion of rural sitting rooms.

96. Mary E. Suter, "A Pictorial History of the Suter Homestead, 1764–1982," unpublished manuscript, Emanuel Suter Collection, Virginia Mennonite Conference Archives, Eastern Mennonite Univ., Harrisonburg, VA.

97. In addition to Bushman's *Refinement* and McMurry's *Families and Farmhouses*, see Myron Stachiw and Nora Pat Small, "Tradition and Transformation: Rural Society and Architectural Change in Nineteenth-century Central Massachusetts," in *Perspectives in Vernacular Architecture*, vol. 3, eds. Thomas Carter and Bernard L. Herman (Columbia: Univ. of Missouri Press, 1989), 135–48.

98. Bushman, *The Refinement of America*, 251. Family weddings were held there throughout the following years. Suter, "Pictorial History."

Chapter 3

1. Emanuel Suter Diary, 5 January 1865, Emanuel Suter Collection, Virginia Mennonite Conference Archives, Eastern Mennonite Univ., Harrisonburg, VA.

2. Ibid., 27 February 1865.

3. References to his work at the Cowden and Wilcox pottery can be found in diaries from February 27 through April 19, 1865, Emanuel Suter Collection, Virginia Mennonite Conference Archives, Eastern Mennonite Univ., Harrisonburg, VA.

4. Bradley Foundry Ledger, SC #2005, Special Collections, Carrier Library, James Madison Univ., Harrisonburg, VA.

5. Describing an architectural feature of this shop, Suter noted in his diary on 14 March 1866: "This morning we drawed the kiln then carried the ware up on the shop loft." Emanuel Suter Collection, Virginia Mennonite Conference Archives, Eastern Mennonite Univ., Harrisonburg, VA.

6. Emanuel Suter Diary, 18 September 1866, Emanuel Suter Collection, Virginia Mennonite Conference Archives, Eastern Mennonite Univ., Harrisonburg, VA.

7. Mary E. Suter, "Explanatory Notes," note to November 20, 1866.

8. Emanuel Suter Diary, 1 November 1866, Emanuel Suter Collection, Virginia Mennonite Conference Archives, Eastern Mennonite Univ., Harrisonburg, VA. Brick for the kiln was hauled from Samuel Driver's on October 18, 1866.

9. Joseph Silber worked for other potters and at various times operated his own shop in Rockingham County. Although Stanley Kaufman suggests that Suter was too busy building the kiln to make ware, and that the ware in the kiln was that of Joseph Silber, I believe that Silber was currently in a business partnership with Suter and that he assisted in burning the kiln. It seems plausible that this ware had been left from the previous shop and unlikely that Silber would haul a load of unfired ware from another shop to burn it in a new kiln. Further evidence that the ware was Suter's lies in the fact that one week after this firing he took a load of ware to a local merchant, suggesting that he was selling his own goods (see diary entry for 22 November 1866). See Stanley A. Kaufman, *Heatwole and Suter Pottery* (Harrisonburg, VA.: Good Printers, 1978), 11. Silber's business relationship with Suter is discussed in detail later in this chapter.

10. Emanuel Suter Diary, 10 December 1866, Emanuel Suter Collection, Virginia Mennonite Conference Archives, Eastern Mennonite Univ., Harrisonburg, VA.

11. In 1871 Suter also built a small kiln on the farm "for burning small ware in," but no photograph or dimensions of this kiln exist. Emanuel Suter Diary, 4 October 1871, Emanuel Suter Collection, Virginia Mennonite Conference Archives, Eastern Mennonite Univ., Harrisonburg, VA.

12. A survey of literature on Pennsylvania potteries reveals no other trapezoidal-shaped kilns in the state. See Jeannette Lasansky, *Central Pennsylvania Redware Pottery, 1780–1904* (Lewisburg: Union County Oral Traditions Project, 1979); Jeannette Lasansky, *Made of Mud: Stoneware Potteries in Central Pennsylvania, 1831–1929* (University Park: the Pennsylvania State Univ. Press, 1979); Elizabeth A. Powell, *Pennsylvania Pottery: Tools and Processes* (Doylestown, PA: Bucks County Historical Society, 1972); Phil Schalten-

brand, *Old Pots: Salt Glazed Stoneware of the Greensboro-New Geneva Region* (Hanover, PA: Everybody's Press, 1977); Phil Schaltenbrand, *Big Ware Turners: The History and Manufacture of Pennsylvania Stoneware, 1720–1920* (Bentleyville, PA: Westerwald Publishing, 2002).

13. 1870 US Census, Rockingham County, VA, industrial and manufacturing schedule, Central Township, p. 2, line 7, Emanuel Suter entry, microfilm, Menno Simons Historical Library, Eastern Mennonite Univ., Harrisonburg, VA.

14. Charles G. Zug III, *Turners and Burners: The Folk Potters of North Carolina* (Chapel Hill: Univ. of North Carolina Press, 1986), 267.

15. 1870 US Census, Rockingham County, Virginia, agriculture schedule, Central Township, p. 7, line 35, Emanuel Suter entry, in-house microfilm, Menno Simons Historical Library, Eastern Mennonite Univ., Harrisonburg, VA.

16. 1880 US Census, Rockingham County, Virginia, industrial and manufacturing schedule, Central Township, p. 1, line 5, Emanuel Suter entry, in-house microfilm, Menno Simons Historical Library, Eastern Mennonite Univ., Harrisonburg, VA.

17. Emanuel Suter Diary, 16 June 1880, Emanuel Suter Collection, Virginia Mennonite Conference Archives, Eastern Mennonite Univ., Harrisonburg, VA.

18. See Evans and Suter, "*A Great Deal of Stone and Earthenware*," 32–36, 45, 50 and Stanley A. Kaufman, *Heatwole and Suter Pottery* (Harrisonburg, VA: Good Printers, 1978), 23, 30.

19. For instance, see bill of L. C. Cootes, 5 August 1884, Emanuel Suter Collection, Virginia Mennonite Conference Archives, Eastern Mennonite Univ., Harrisonburg, VA.

20. Paul R. Mullins, "Traditional Pottery Adaptation in the Shenandoah Valley: The Diaries and Business Records of Emanuel Suter" delivered at the Council for Northeast Archaeology, 1989, TMs [photocopy], 8, Emanuel Suter Collection, Virginia Mennonite Conference Archives, Eastern Mennonite Univ., Harrisonburg, VA.

21. Emanuel Suter Diary, Memoranda page, 1866, Emanuel Suter Collection, Virginia Mennonite Conference Archives, Eastern Mennonite Univ., Harrisonburg, VA.

22. J. H. Plecker to Emanuel Suter, 17 April 1878, Staunton, VA, Emanuel Suter Collection, Virginia Mennonite Conference Archives, Eastern Mennonite Univ., Harrisonburg, VA.

23. A review of many orders and bills for ware as well as the pots themselves demonstrates that the variety of Suter's forms was immense. Future studies of the Emanuel Suter potteries should concentrate on identifying and cataloging as many known examples of his ware as possible. At present the most comprehensive pictorial work is Evans and Suter's "*A Great Deal of Stone and Earthenware.*"

24. Zug, *Turners and Burners*, 287, 289. Zug points out that in North Carolina traditional pottery was used into the twentieth century.

25. The sizes and types of Suter's wares were determined from a sampling of twenty-five bills of ware ranging from 1867 to 1896.

26. Evidence from bills of ware and existing pieces suggest this to be the case. See Evans and Suter, "*A Great Deal of Stone and Earthenware*," 89.

27. In the photograph of the New Erection Pottery, one gallon crocks can be seen stacked on the loading platform to the left and inside the door on the right of the image.

28. See Zug, *Turners and Burners*, 311–15. He quotes Mrs. J. W. Gentry as saying: "You wanted it [milk] in something that's pretty big at the top so the cream'd rise to the top. An you could just skim off that cream" (312).

29. McCorkle Brothers to Emanuel Suter, Middlebrook, VA, 2 January 1877, Emanuel Suter Collection, Virginia Mennonite Conference Archives, Eastern Mennonite Univ., Harrisonburg, VA.

30. Emanuel Suter Diary, 1869, Emanuel Suter Collection, Virginia Mennonite Conference Archives, Eastern Mennonite Univ., Harrisonburg, VA.

31. A bill of ware got of Jacob D. Suter, March 18, 1869, Emanuel Suter Collection, Virginia Mennonite Conference Archives, Eastern Mennonite Univ., Harrisonburg, VA.

32. These pitchers were also referred to as "large" and "small" in at least one bill. See "A Bill of ware got of Jacob D. Suter," 18 March 1869, Emanuel Suter Collection, Virginia Mennonite Conference Archives, Eastern Mennonite Univ., Harrisonburg, VA.

33. This seems to be an early date for the use of molds in the Shenandoah Valley pottery tradition; however, John D. Heatwole and John G. Schweinfurt produced molded handles.

34. Emanuel Suter Diary, 12 August 1867, Emanuel Suter Collection, Virginia Mennonite Conference Archives, Eastern Mennonite Univ., Harrisonburg, VA.

35. Emanuel Suter Account Books, Emanuel Suter Collection, Virginia Mennonite Conference Archives, Eastern Mennonite Univ., Harrisonburg, VA.

36. Diary of David Irenaeus Suter, 19 June 1890, Private Collection.

37. "Today I fixed for making pipe & made pipe, turned some pots this evening." Emanuel Suter Diary, 25 January 1870. "Today James Ford & myself were making tile." Emanuel Suter Diary, 26 January 1870, and so forth. Emanuel Suter Collection, Virginia Mennonite Conference Archives, Eastern Mennonite Univ., Harrisonburg, VA. The first kiln of ware fired at the Harrisonburg Steam Pottery, however, was earthenware.

38. J. M. Quarles to E. Suter & Son, Staunton, VA, 23 October 1888, Emanuel Suter Collection, Virginia Mennonite Conference Archives, Eastern Mennonite Univ., Harrisonburg, VA.

39. The large call for drain tile also indicates another reason for Suter's adoption of a tile press.

40. These pieces are also referred to as chimney thimbles, stove pipe thimbles, stove tubes, and stove collars.

41. For instance, see bill of ware for M. C. Freiber, Staunton, VA, 25 April 1888, Emanuel Suter Collection, Virginia Mennonite Conference Archives, Eastern Mennonite Univ., Harrisonburg, VA. Freiber bought a lot of eight, nine, and ten-inch flower pots and specified saucers for each size.

42. Mary J. Baldwin to Emanuel Suter & Son, 20 December 1888, Staunton, VA, Emanuel Suter Collection, Virginia Mennonite Conference Archives, Eastern Mennonite Univ., Harrisonburg, VA. As late as 1891 (after the razing of the New Erection Pottery, but before the opening of the Harrisonburg Steam Pottery), Suter received an order for "500 5 inch nourishers for potted plants." Steward C. Miller, Western State Lunatic Asylum, to Emanuel Suter, 12 January 1891, Staunton, VA, Emanuel Suter Collection, Virginia Mennonite Conference Archives, Eastern Mennonite Univ., Harrisonburg, VA.

43. On 3 September 1886 Suter noted in his diary: "We commenced on a flower pot bill [for] Freiber & Coiner of 20,000." Emanuel Suter Collection, Virginia Mennonite Conference Archives, Eastern Mennonite Univ., Harrisonburg, VA.

44. Emanuel Suter Diary, 10 March 1886, Emanuel Suter Collection, Virginia Mennonite Conference Archives, Eastern Mennonite Univ., Harrisonburg, VA. This brought the number of kilns at the shop to three—two small ones (one was built in 1871) and the large one.

45. For instance, see diary entries for 13 September, 21 September, and 27 September, 1886.

46. A common diary entry for this period reads: "To day I was turning flower pots all day." Emanuel Suter Diary, 7 September 1886, Emanuel Suter Collection, Virginia Mennonite Conference Archives, Eastern Mennonite Univ., Harrisonburg, VA. Regarding his work on Sundays, on 12 September 1886, a Sunday, Suter recorded: "To day I worked in the pottery all day burned a kiln of flower pots, finished at ten tonight." Upon rereading this entry at a later date, Suter noted at the bottom of this page: "The above must be a mistake as I never did work on Sunday. The work mentioned was done on Saturday, day before."

47. Suter's account book for 1886 shows that Reuben was "turning flower pots" daily in September and October.

48. Isaac Good, Account Book, private collection, 61.

49. Emanuel Suter Diary, Memoranda page, 1886, Emanuel Suter Collection, Virginia Mennonite Conference Archives, Eastern Mennonite Univ., Harrisonburg, VA.

50. Emanuel Suter Diary, 5 November 1886, Emanuel Suter Collection, Virginia Mennonite Conference Archives, Eastern Mennonite Univ., Harrisonburg, VA.

51. Suter noted: "I helped to burn a stone ware kiln[,] I think this is the last one that will be burned here, after this the pottery will be in Harrisonburg." Emanuel Suter Diary, 7 August 1890, Emanuel Suter Collection, Virginia Mennonite Conference Archives, Eastern Mennonite Univ., Harrisonburg, VA.

52. Emanuel Suter Diary, 30 December 1874, Emanuel Suter Collection, Virginia Mennonite Conference Archives, Eastern Mennonite Univ., Harrisonburg, VA.

53. J. L. Thompson to Emanuel Suter, 5 April 1875, Dayton, VA, Emanuel Suter Collection, Virginia Mennonite Conference Archives, Eastern Mennonite Univ., Harrisonburg, VA. On 26 April 1878, Ed. S. Conrad wrote to Suter: "Please bring me a vase like the large ones I brought with me yesterday, the next time you come to town." Emanuel Suter Collection, Virginia Mennonite Conference Archives, Eastern Mennonite Univ., Harrisonburg, VA.

54. See Evans and Suter, *"A Great Deal of Stone and Earthenware,"* 85–86.

55. Sabine Jervis-Edwards to Emanuel Suter, 15 January 1884, Harrisonburg, VA, Emanuel Suter Collection, Virginia Mennonite Conference Archives, Eastern Mennonite Univ., Harrisonburg, VA.

56. Kaufman, *Heatwole and Suter Pottery,* 42.

57. Suter owned an advertising catalog from the Philadelphia Terra-Cotta Works, which illustrates decorative vessels of this type.

58. Emanuel Suter Diary, 26 January 1887, Emanuel Suter Collection, Virginia Mennonite Conference Archives, Eastern Mennonite Univ., Harrisonburg, VA.

59. Comstock, *Pottery of the Shenandoah Valley Region*, 50.

60. Emanuel Suter Diary, 29 March 1865, Emanuel Suter Collection, Virginia Mennonite Conference Archives, Eastern Mennonite Univ., Harrisonburg, VA.

61. M. Luther Heisey, "The Makers of Pottery in Lancaster County," in *Papers Read before the Lancaster County Historical Society*, vol. 1, nos. 4 and 5 (1946): 117–28.

62. Comstock, *Pottery of the Shenandoah Valley Region*, 52.

63. Emanuel Suter Diary, August 26, 1865, Emanuel Suter Collection, Virginia Mennonite Conference Archives, Eastern Mennonite Univ., Harrisonburg, VA.

64. Samuel Shacklett Day Book, January 12, 1866, 115, SC #4040, Special Collections, Carrier Library, James Madison Univ., Harrisonburg, VA.

65. For instance, Suter received five kegs of lead from Davis, Chambers Lead Company of Pittsburgh, Pennsylvania in August of 1886.

66. Emanuel Suter Diary, 19 May 1876, Emanuel Suter Collection, Virginia Mennonite Conference Archives, Eastern Mennonite Univ., Harrisonburg, VA.

67. Rudolf Hainbach, *Pottery Decorating, translated from the German*, 2nd ed. (London: Scott, Greenwood & Son, 1924), 95.

68. Emanuel Suter Diary, 19 March 1867, Emanuel Suter Collection, Virginia Mennonite Conference Archives, Eastern Mennonite Univ., Harrisonburg, VA.

69. See Evans and Suter's *"A Great Deal of Stone and Earthenware"* for comparison pieces.

70. See Evans and Suter, *"A Great Deal of Stone and Earthenware,"* 32–37.

71. Letter from D. H. Martz, 6 August 1879, Emanuel Suter Collection, Virginia Mennonite Conference Archives, Eastern Mennonite Univ., Harrisonburg, VA.

72. Compare Evans and Suter, *"A Great Deal of Stone and Earthenware,"* image 54, p. 49, with numerous examples from Matthew R. Miller, *Decorated Stoneware of Cowden and the Stoneware Potteries of Harrisburg Pennsylvania, 1852–1924* (Shermans Dale, PA: Self-published, 2001), 95–118.

73. Comstock, *Pottery of the Shenandoah Valley Region*, 22.

74. Emanuel Suter Diary, 15 November 1865, memoranda page, Emanuel Suter Collection, Virginia Mennonite Conference Archives, Eastern Mennonite Univ., Harrisonburg, VA.

75. Emanuel Suter Account Book, Emanuel Suter Collection, Virginia Mennonite Conference Archives, Eastern Mennonite Univ., Harrisonburg, VA, 28.

76. *Rockingham Register* (Harrisonburg, VA), February 20, 1868.

77. Emanuel Suter Diary, 14 June 1867, Emanuel Suter Collection, Virginia Mennonite Conference Archives, Eastern Mennonite Univ., Harrisonburg, VA.

78. Significantly, the census indicates that Joseph Silber, "potter," lived adjacent to Woods. It is not unreasonable to conjecture that this was the period of the "Woods & Silber" partnership.

79. Emanuel Suter Account Book, 1874, Emanuel Suter Collection, Virginia Mennonite Conference Archives, Eastern Mennonite Univ., Harrisonburg, VA. Rockingham County Deed Book 2, p. 309. For Suter's mention of Airy see the diary entries for 5–6 November 1877.

80. Emanuel Suter Diaries, February 1889, Emanuel Suter Collection, Virginia Mennonite Conference Archives, Eastern Mennonite Univ., Harrisonburg, VA.

81. Emanuel Suter Collection, Virginia Mennonite Conference Archives, Eastern Mennonite Univ., Harrisonburg, VA.

82. Ibid.

83. Emanuel Suter Diary, 19 May 1876, Emanuel Suter Collection, Virginia Mennonite Conference Archives, Eastern Mennonite Univ., Harrisonburg, VA. This is the only mention in the diaries of using clay materials from this particular site .

84. Ibid., 7 August 1868 and 17 November 1868.

85. Eugene Suter Interview by Elmer Smith and John Stewart, July 1963. Blue Ridge Institute, Ferrum College, Ferrum, VA.

86. Comstock, *The Pottery of the Shenandoah Valley Region*, 28.

87. Emanuel Suter Diary, back cover, 1864–1865, Emanuel Suter Collection, Virginia Mennonite Conference Archives, Eastern Mennonite Univ., Harrisonburg, VA.

88. See Jeanette Lasansky, *Made of Mud: Stoneware Potteries in Central Pennsylvania, 1831–1929* (University Park, PA: Pennsylvania State Univ. Press, 1979), 10–11; Arthur E. James, *The Potters and Potteries of Chester County, Pennsylvania*, 2nd ed. (Exton, PA: Schiffer Publishing Ltd., 1978), 26; Phil Schaltenbrand, *Big Ware Turners: The History and Manufacture of Pennsylvania Stoneware, 1720–1920* (Bentleyville, PA: Westerwald Publishing, 2002), 78–79.

89. Emanuel Suter Diary, 17 June 1867, and Emanuel Suter Diary, 14 April 1869, Emanuel Suter Collection, Virginia Mennonite Conference Archives, Eastern Mennonite Univ., Harrisonburg, VA.

90. Ibid., 18–19 May 1869.

91. Ibid., 22 and 27 May 1869.

92. Ibid., 3 June 1869.

93. Ibid., 22 December, 1882.

94. Ibid., 28 December 1882 and 31 January–1 February 1883.

95. See Comstock, *The Pottery of the Shenandoah Valley Region*, 30, for an image of Valley potter John Schweinfurt's potter's ribs.

96. Emanuel Suter Diary, 7 February 1871 and 7 January 1893, Emanuel Suter Collection, Virginia Mennonite Conference Archives, Eastern Mennonite Univ., Harrisonburg, VA.

97. Ibid., 12 February 1866

98. Ibid., 20–21 February 1866.

99. Mary E. Suter, "Explanatory Notes," note for 12 February 1866.

100. Emanuel Suter Diary, 25 January 1870, Emanuel Suter Collection, Virginia Mennonite Conference Archives, Eastern Mennonite Univ., Harrisonburg, VA.

101. Ibid., 6 May 1870.

102. Ibid., 31 July 1878.

103. Ibid., 24 August 1878.

104. Edward Dobson, *A Rudimentary Treatise on the Manufacture of Bricks and Tiles containing an Outline of the Principles of Brickmaking*, 11th ed. (London: Crosby Lockwood and Son, 1903), 205.

105. Emanuel Suter Diary, 5–6 March 1883, Emanuel Suter Collection, Virginia Mennonite Conference Archives, Eastern Mennonite Univ., Harrisonburg, VA.

106. Mary E. Suter, "Explanatory Notes," note for 10 August 1866.

107. Suter's diaries reveal that there were steam saw mills in the area as early as the 1870s. Undoubtedly some were in existence prior to that time.

108. Emanuel Suter Diary, 26 January 1884, Emanuel Suter Collection, Virginia Mennonite Conference Archives, Eastern Mennonite Univ., Harrisonburg, VA.

109. Ibid., 6 February 1884.

110. Mary E. Suter, "Explanatory Notes," note for 30 January 1884.

111. *Rockingham Register* (Harrisonburg, VA), April 24, 1884.

112. Emanuel Suter Diary, 9 April 1885, Emanuel Suter Collection, Virginia Mennonite Conference Archives, Eastern Mennonite Univ., Harrisonburg, VA.

113. Emanuel Suter Diary, 30 March1885, Emanuel Suter Collection, Virginia Mennonite Conference Archives, Eastern Mennonite Univ., Harrisonburg, VA.

114. David Irenaeus Suter Diary, 19 August 1890, private collection.

115. Insurance Policy, The West Rockingham Mutual Fire Insurance Co., 10 June 1879, Emanuel Suter Collection, Virginia Mennonite Conference Archives, Eastern Mennonite Univ., Harrisonburg, VA.

116. Emanuel Suter Diary, 7 April 1875, Emanuel Suter Collection, Virginia Mennonite Conference Archives, Eastern Mennonite Univ., Harrisonburg, VA.

117. Suter, *Memories of Yesteryear*, 50.

118. Emanuel Suter Diary, 4 March 1884, Emanuel Suter Collection, Virginia Mennonite Conference Archives, Eastern Mennonite Univ., Harrisonburg, VA.

119. D.I. Suter noted, for instance, on 7 May 1890: "Today I helped to grind 83 balls of clay in the cellar." David Irenaeus Suter Diary, private collection.

120. Emanuel Suter Diary, 1 May 1867, Emanuel Suter Collection, Virginia Mennonite Conference Archives, Eastern Mennonite Univ., Harrisonburg, VA.

121. Suter, *Memories of Yesteryear*, 51.

122. Emanuel Suter Diary, 17 January 1893, Emanuel Suter Collection, Virginia Mennonite Conference Archives, Eastern Mennonite Univ., Harrisonburg, VA.

123. Ibid., 31 August 1867.

124. Emanuel Suter Account Book, Emanuel Suter Collection, Virginia Mennonite Conference Archives, Eastern Mennonite Univ., Harrisonburg, VA.

125. *Rockingham Register* (Harrisonburg, VA), September 2, 1875.

126. Sale Bill, New Erection Steam Pottery, 1886, Emanuel Suter Collection, Virginia Mennonite Conference Archives, Eastern Mennonite Univ., Harrisonburg, VA.

127. F. M. Stinespring to Emanuel Suter, 6 September 1876, Singers Glen, VA, Emanuel Suter Collection, Virginia Mennonite Conference Archives, Eastern Mennonite Univ., Harrisonburg, VA.

128. F. M. Stinespring to Emanuel Suter, 16 August 1876, Singers Glen, VA, Emanuel Suter Collection, Virginia Mennonite Conference Archives, Eastern Mennonite Univ., Harrisonburg, VA.

129. F. M. Stinespring to Emanuel Suter, 26 May 1878, Singers Glen, VA, Emanuel Suter Collection, Virginia Mennonite Conference Archives, Eastern Mennonite Univ., Harrisonburg, VA.

130. J. W. Minnich to Emanuel Suter, 4 June 1877, Dale Enterprise, VA, Emanuel Suter Collection, Virginia Mennonite Conference Archives, Eastern Mennonite Univ., Harrisonburg, VA.

131. Plecker also operated a store in Staunton, VA, a city that was on the rail line. Suter undoubtedly understood the importance of gaining this man's business.

132. J. H. Plecker to Emanuel Suter, 27 September 1869, Spring Hill, VA, Emanuel Suter Collection, Virginia Mennonite Conference Archives, Eastern Mennonite Univ., Harrisonburg, VA. In this case Suter offered to take the goods hoping to establish a business relationship.

133. Suter also sold ware to a Mr. Craig and to the merchants Lipscomb & Somerville as well as furnishing flower pots to the Western State Lunatic Asylum and Mary Baldwin's Seminary.

134. J. H. Plecker to Emanuel Suter, 5 January 1880, Staunton, VA, Emanuel Suter Collection, Virginia Mennonite Conference Archives, Eastern Mennonite Univ., Harrisonburg, VA.

135. Emanuel Suter to Reuben Suter, 10 July 1879, Harrisonburg, VA, Emanuel Suter Collection, Virginia Mennonite Conference Archives, Eastern Mennonite Univ., Harrisonburg, VA.

136. J. E. Heatwole to Emanuel Suter, 12 June 1877, Dillon's Run, Hampshire County, WV, Emanuel Suter Collection, Virginia Mennonite Conference Archives, Eastern Mennonite Univ., Harrisonburg, VA. For information on the Strasburg and Winchester potters see A. H. Rice and John Baer Stoudt, *The Shenandoah Pottery* (Strasburg, VA: Shenandoah Publishing House, 1929); H. E. Comstock, introduction to *Folk Pottery of the Shenandoah Valley* by William E. Wiltshire, III (New York: E. P. Dutton, 1975); Comstock, *The Pottery of the Shenandoah Valley Region*.

137. H. M. Baker to Emanuel Suter, 20 August 1875, Emanuel Suter Collection, Virginia Mennonite Conference Archives, Eastern Mennonite Univ., Harrisonburg, VA.

138. Emanuel Suter Diary, 30–31 August 1875, Emanuel Suter Collection, Virginia Mennonite Conference Archives, Eastern Mennonite Univ., Harrisonburg, VA.

139. H. M. Baker to Emanuel Suter, 1 August 1879, Emanuel Suter Collection, Virginia Mennonite Conference Archives, Eastern Mennonite Univ., Harrisonburg, VA.

140. H. M. Baker to Emanuel Suter, 13 August 1879, Emanuel Suter Collection, Virginia Mennonite Conference Archives, Eastern Mennonite Univ., Harrisonburg, VA.

141. There is no evidence that Suter and Baker ever met face to face.

142. Lefevre to Emanuel Suter, 11 August 1879, Winchester, VA, Emanuel Suter Collection, Virginia Mennonite Conference Archives, Eastern Mennonite Univ., Harrisonburg, VA.

143. H. M. Baker to Emanuel Suter, 27 December 1879, Winchester, VA, Emanuel Suter Collection, Virginia Mennonite Conference Archives, Eastern Mennonite Univ., Harrisonburg, VA.

144. See John H. Sonner Account Book, Winterthur Library, Joseph Downs Collection of Manuscripts and Printed Ephemera, Doc. 378.

145. John A. Burrison and Charles Zug discuss the tendency of potters to hire seasonal workers in Georgia and North Carolina respectively. See Burrison, *Brothers in Clay: The Story of Georgia Folk Pottery* (Athens: Univ. of Georgia Press, 1983), 35, and Zug, *Turners and Burners*, 262–64.

146. Joseph Gaines died at age sixty-seven in December of 1905. A note on his funeral reported that "before the war he was a slave, owned by the Maupins on Linville Creek." "Funeral of Joseph Gaines," *Harrisonburg Daily News* (Harrisonburg, VA), January 3, 1906.

147. Emanuel Suter Diary, 13 February 1871 and 19 May 1871, Emanuel Suter Collection, Virginia Mennonite Conference Archives, Eastern Mennonite Univ., Harrisonburg, VA.

148. Mary E. Suter, *Memories of Yesteryear*, 56. Also see Emanuel Suter Account Books, Emanuel Suter Collection, Virginia Mennonite Conference Archives, Eastern Mennonite Univ., Harrisonburg, VA.

149. Emanuel Suter Diary, 11 November 1868, Emanuel Suter Collection, Virginia Mennonite Conference Archives, Eastern Mennonite Univ., Harrisonburg, VA.

150. Emanuel Suter Diary, Emanuel Suter Collection, Virginia Mennonite Conference Archives, Eastern Mennonite Univ., Harrisonburg, VA.

151. Ibid., 13 April 1869.

152. 1870 US Census, Augusta County, VA, industrial and manufacturing schedule, Charles Binsfeld entry, microfilm, Menno Simons Historical Library, Eastern Mennonite Univ., Harrisonburg, VA.

153. Emanuel Suter Diary, 21 May 1870, Emanuel Suter Collection, Virginia Mennonite Conference Archives, Eastern Mennonite Univ., Harrisonburg, VA.

154. For instance: "To day myself & John W. Ford sowed clover seed & worked in the potter shop." Emanuel Suter Diary, 6 March 1876, Emanuel Suter Collection, Virginia Mennonite Conference Archives, Eastern Mennonite Univ., Harrisonburg, VA. Ford is listed as a twenty-one-year-old laborer living next to John D. Heatwole in the 1870 census. He was married to Heatwole's daughter Nancy. It is reasonable to assume that Ford learned the pottery craft from Heatwole; although he is listed in the 1870 census as a laborer, by 1880 he was listed as a potter. See Evans and Suter, *"A Great Deal of Stone and Earthenware,"* 19, and Comstock, *Pottery of the Shenandoah Valley Region*, 403.

155. Emanuel Suter Diary, 25 July 1876, Emanuel Suter Collection, Virginia Mennonite Conference Archives, Eastern Mennonite Univ., Harrisonburg, VA.

156. Emanuel Suter Account Book, Emanuel Suter Collection, Virginia Mennonite Conference Archives, Eastern Mennonite Univ., Harrisonburg, VA.

157. Emanuel Suter Diary, 19 October 1865, Emanuel Suter Collection, Virginia Mennonite Conference Archives, Eastern Mennonite Univ., Harrisonburg, VA.

158. A note in *The Old Commonwealth* (Harrisonburg, VA), April 25, 1866, states that "Messrs. Heatwole & Silber" are making large quantities of stoneware on Dry River.

159. *Rockingham Register* (Harrisonburg, VA), September 6, 1866.

160. Emanuel Suter Diary, 14 November 1866 and 6 February 1867, Emanuel Suter Collection, Virginia Mennonite Conference Archives, Eastern Mennonite Univ., Harrisonburg, VA.

161. Ibid., 30 October 1867.

162. Rockingham County, VA, Records, Marriage License, December 26, 1867.

163. Emanuel Suter Diary, 14 September 1874, Emanuel Suter Collection, Virginia Mennonite Conference Archives, Eastern Mennonite Univ., Harrisonburg, VA.

164. For the details of Silber's time in Highland County, Virginia, see the report on Kent

Botkin's research: "Highland Potter's Story Unearthed," *The Recorder* (Monterey, VA), March 14, 2013, 7–8.

165. Emanuel Suter Diary, 12–14 October 1874, Emanuel Suter Collection, Virginia Mennonite Conference Archives, Eastern Mennonite Univ., Harrisonburg, VA.

166. Ibid., 14 June 1875.

167. Rockingham County, VA, Records, Deed Book 13, 439.

168. J. Payne vs. Joseph Silber, Rockingham County, VA, Chancery Court Records, and John Cromer's Adm. vs. Daniel Good's Adm., Rockingham County, VA, Chancery Court Records.

169. Comstock, *Pottery of the Shenandoah Valley Region*, 467.

170. Mt. Clinton Voter Registers, 1867–1901, Special Collections, Carrier Library, James Madison Univ., Harrisonburg, VA. Karle also appears in Suter's accounts from the 1870s; he helped with the harvest. For more information on Otto Karle as a potter see Scott Hamilton Suter, "Otto Karle: A Previously Unknown Shenandoah Valley Potter," in *Ceramics in America 2005*, ed. Robert Hunter (Milwaukee: Chipstone Foundation, 2005), 229–32, and Evans and Suter, "*A Great Deal of Stone and Earthenware*," 23–24.

171. Emanuel Suter Diary, 31 March 1868, Emanuel Suter Collection, Virginia Mennonite Conference Archives, Eastern Mennonite Univ., Harrisonburg, VA.

172. Ibid., 2 May 1871 and 22 August 1871.

173. Suter's records show that for the six days that Good worked in February of 1886 he was paid seventy-five cents per day to turn flower pots. When Good came back to work in March he began to receive the dollar-a-day wage.

174. 1880 US Census, Rockingham County, VA, industrial and manufacturing schedule.

175. John H. Sonner Account Book, Winterthur Library, Joseph Downs Collection of Manuscripts and Printed Ephemera, Doc. 378.

176. Emanuel Suter Account Book, 42, Emanuel Suter Collection, Virginia Mennonite Conference Archives, Eastern Mennonite Univ., Harrisonburg, VA.

177. Good's account book shows credit for Suter in the amount of $ 79.52. Our addition differs by forty-seven cents. Isaac Good's account books are privately owned.

178. Good's parents lived on a farm adjacent to the Suter property.

179. Emanuel Suter Diary, 14 February 1873, Emanuel Suter Collection, Virginia Mennonite Conference Archives, Eastern Mennonite Univ., Harrisonburg, VA.

180. Emanuel Suter Collection, Virginia Mennonite Conference Archives, Eastern Mennonite Univ., Harrisonburg, VA.

181. Emanuel Suter Diary, 8–22 March 1880, Emanuel Suter Collection, Virginia Mennonite Conference Archives, Eastern Mennonite Univ., Harrisonburg, VA.

182. Ibid., 8 September 1883.

183. For a thorough discussion of owner-worker relationships at North Carolina potteries see Zug, *Turners and Burners*, 262–68.

184. Emanuel Suter Diary, 16 and 27 April 1877, Emanuel Suter Collection, Virginia Mennonite Conference Archives, Eastern Mennonite Univ., Harrisonburg, VA.

185. Emanuel Suter Diary, 3 October 1877, Emanuel Suter Collection, Virginia Mennonite Conference Archives, Eastern Mennonite Univ., Harrisonburg, VA.

186. Emanuel Suter Account Book, 3 September 1886, Emanuel Suter Collection, Virginia Mennonite Conference Archives, Eastern Mennonite Univ., Harrisonburg, VA.

187. Emanuel Suter Diary, 4 May 1888, Emanuel Suter Collection, Virginia Mennonite Conference Archives, Eastern Mennonite Univ., Harrisonburg, VA.

188. Ibid., 31 May 1888.

189. Ibid., 5 July 1888.

190. Ibid., 25 July 1888.

191. Ibid., 24 September 1888.

192. Ibid., 26 October 1888.

193. Ibid., 6 September 1889.

194. Ibid., 11 September 1889

195. Ibid., 4 November 1889.

196. David Irenaeus Suter Diary, 17 March 1890, private collection.

197. Ibid., 28–29 April 1890.

198. Emanuel Suter Diary, 7 May 1890.

199. Ibid., 29 May 1890.

200. David Irenaeus Suter Diary, 29 May 1890, private collection.

201. Emanuel Suter Diary, 10 June 1890, Emanuel Suter Collection, Virginia Mennonite Conference Archives, Eastern Mennonite Univ., Harrisonburg, VA.

202. David Irenaeus Suter Diary, 10 June 1890, private collection.

203. Emanuel Suter Diary, 13 June 1890, Emanuel Suter Collection, Virginia Mennonite Conference Archives, Eastern Mennonite Univ., Harrisonburg, VA.

204. David Irenaeus Suter Diary, 13 June 1890, private collection.

Chapter 4

1. Emanuel Suter Diary, 10 June 1890, Emanuel Suter Collection, Virginia Mennonite Conference Archives, Eastern Mennonite Univ., Harrisonburg, VA.

2. See Howard Mumford Jones, *The Age of Energy: Varieties of American Experience, 1865–1915* (New York: The Viking Press, 1970) and Alan Trachtenberg, *The Incorporation of America: Culture and Society in the Gilded Age* (New York: Hill and Wang, 1982).

3. Trachtenberg, *The Incorporation of America*, 3.

4. "Are We Booming?," *Rockingham Register* (Harrisonburg, VA), April 17, 1891.

5. Charter Book I, Rockingham County, 216–17.

6. "A Great Lot Sale," *Rockingham Register* (Harrisonburg, VA), August 22, 1890.

7. Advertisement, *Rockingham Register* (Harrisonburg, VA), August 8, 1890.

8. "A Great Lot Sale," *Rockingham Register* (Harrisonburg, VA), August 22, 1890.

9. "Lot Sale," *Rockingham Register* (Harrisonburg, VA), December 5, 1890.

10. "Death of Wm. Sherratt," *Rockingham Register* (Harrisonburg, VA), November 4, 1892.

11. Rockingham County, VA, Chancery Causes, 1781–1913, Harrisonburg Land and Improvement Co. v. Rockingham Pottery Co, 1901–022, Local Government Records Collection, Rockingham Court Records, The Library of Virginia, Richmond, VA. For a complete account of the life of this enterprise see Scott Hamilton Suter, "'Unless Delayed by Un-

foreseen Circumstances': A Tale of a Shenandoah Valley Industrial Pottery," forthcoming in *Ceramics in America 2018*, ed. Robert Hunter (Milwaukee: Chipstone Foundation, 2018), 142-69.

12. "An Important Pottery Deal," *Rockingham Register* (Harrisonburg, VA), April 8, 1892.

13. "Fire at the Pottery," *Rockingham Register* (Harrisonburg, VA), July 22, 1892.

14. Ibid.

15. Rockingham County (VA) Chancery Causes, 1781–1913, Harrisonburg Land and Improvement Co. vs. Rockingham Pottery Co, 1901–022, Local Government Records Collection, Rockingham Court Records, The Library of Virginia, Richmond, VA.

16. *Rockingham Register* (Harrisonburg, VA), June 23, 1893.

17. For a study of how Harrisonburg did evolve after the turn of the century see Scott Hamilton Suter and David Ehrenpreis, "Boosterism and Heritage: Postcards of Harrisonburg, 1900–1915," in *Picturing Harrisonburg: Visions of a Shenandoah Valley City Since 1828*, ed. David Ehrenpreis (Staunton, VA: George F. Thompson Publishing, 2017), 89–118.

18. Quoted in Comstock, *The Pottery of the Shenandoah Valley Region*, 478.

19. Ibid., 479.

20. Ibid., 480.

21. Ibid., 480–81.

22. Charter Book I, Rockingham County, VA, 227-29.

23. Emanuel Suter Diary, 16 June 1890, Emanuel Suter Collection, Virginia Mennonite Conference Archives, Eastern Mennonite Univ., Harrisonburg, VA.

24. Suter's older brother Gabriel lived in Zanesville, and he stayed with him during this visit. Gabriel did not work in a pottery there, but the two had corresponded about clay and prices.

25. Emanuel Suter Diary, 21 June 1890, Emanuel Suter Collection, Virginia Mennonite Conference Archives, Eastern Mennonite Univ., Harrisonburg, VA.

26. Ibid., 23 June 1890.

27. Report of Emanuel Suter's 1890 Trip in the Interest of the Harrisonburg Steam Pottery, Emanuel Suter Collection, Virginia Mennonite Conference Archives, Eastern Mennonite Univ., Harrisonburg, VA. The manuscript is damaged; words and letters enclosed in brackets indicate my additions. Notes taken by Suter in a memo book during the trip provide a basis for filling in the damaged parts of the manuscript.

28. The Roseville company and individuals Suter mentions are: "Kildow, Dugan & Co. (L. S. Kildow, B. A. Dugan, C. L. Williams, and J. W. McCoy), manufacturers of pudding pans, frying pans, cooking crocks, coffee pots and general hollow superior stoneware. Austin Lowery, manufacturer of stoneware, plaster dies . . . J. D. H. Parrott, manufacturer of steam and horse clay crushers for potteries and all clay products." *Biographical and Historical Memoirs of Muskingum County, Ohio: Embracing and Authentic and Comprehensive Account of the Chief Events and History of the County and a Record of the Lives of Many of the Most Worthy Families and Individuals* (Chicago: The Godspeed Publishing Co., 1892), 323–24.

29. See Phil Schaltenbrand, *Old Pots: Salt-Glazed Stoneware of the Greensboro-New Geneva Region* (Hanover, PA: Everybody's Press, 1977), 27; Phil Schaltenbrand, *Stoneware of*

Southwestern Pennsylvania (Pittsburgh: Univ. of Pittsburgh Press, 1996); Elmer L. Smith, *Pottery: A Utilitarian Folk Craft* (Lebanon, PA: Applied Arts Publishers, 1972), 13. See Emanuel Suter Diary, 18 June 1890, Emanuel Suter Collection, Virginia Mennonite Conference Archives, Eastern Mennonite Univ., Harrisonburg, VA.

30. Report of Emanuel Suter's 1890 Trip in the Interest of the Harrisonburg Steam Pottery, Emanuel Suter Collection, Virginia Mennonite Conference Archives, Eastern Mennonite Univ., Harrisonburg, VA.

31. Ibid. In his notebook from the journey Suter recorded: "Power used in this pottery, 35 horse, this runs presses, pug mills, lathes, three turning wheels, one giger [jigger]." See unlabeled notebook, Emanuel Suter Collection, Virginia Mennonite Conference Archives, Eastern Mennonite Univ., Harrisonburg, VA.

32. Miller, *Decorated Stoneware of Cowden*, 37 and 139. Suter wrote to his wife: "I obtained valuable information at Harrisburg about the pottery. I found in Mr. Cowden a gentleman and his wife a lady." Emanuel Suter to Elizabeth Suter, July 26, 1890, Emanuel Suter Collection, Virginia Mennonite Conference Archives, Eastern Mennonite Univ., Harrisonburg, VA.

33. Emanuel Suter Diary, 30 July 1890, Emanuel Suter Collection, Virginia Mennonite Conference Archives, Eastern Mennonite Univ., Harrisonburg, VA.

34. John E. Kille documents the adaptive methods of M. Perine and Sons in "Distinguishing Marks and Flowering Designs: Baltimore's Utilitarian Stoneware Industry," in *Ceramics in America 2005*, ed. Robert Hunter (Hanover: Chipstone Foundation, 2005), 126–27.

35. Jane Perkins Claney, *Rockingham Ware in American Culture, 1830–1930: Reading Historical Artifacts* (Hanover: Univ. Press of New England, 2004), 46–47.

36. Emanuel Suter Diary, 31 March 1891, Emanuel Suter Collection, Virginia Mennonite Conference Archives, Eastern Mennonite Univ., Harrisonburg, VA.

37. Ibid., 3 April 1891. Rose, Ernst, Furman, and Ryan were all clay miners who furnished clay for many potteries in the mid-Atlantic region.

38. For the story of that industrial pottery see Suter, "'Unless Delayed by Unforeseen Circumstances,'" and *Rockingham Register* (Harrisonburg, VA), October 3, 1890. Also see obituary for William Sherratt, *Rockingham Register*, November 4, 1892.

39. The Harrisonburg Steam Pottery was located on Primary State Highway 42 approximately .2 miles north of the intersection with Edom Road in Harrisonburg. The site is currently occupied by James Madison University offices in a building originally constructed in 1978. At the time of that construction a large quantity of sherds and kiln furniture were recovered. There has been no further archaeological investigation at the site. See Stanley A. Kaufman, *Heatwole and Suter Pottery* (Harrisonburg, VA: Good Printers, 1978), 12. A Sanborn Insurance map from 1891 shows a rectangular structure situated north and south and parallel to the B & O Railroad tracks. The single kiln is identified as a down draught kiln eight feet high in a kiln room with a brick floor.

40. Rockingham County (VA) Chancery Causes, 1781–1913, W. N. Sprinkel vs. J. P. Houck, C. A. Sprinkel vs. J. P. Houck, and J. P. Houck v. C. A. Sprinkel, 1901–072, Local Government Records Collection, Rockingham Court Records, The Library of Virginia, Richmond, VA, 1189–1190.

41. Emanuel Suter Diary, 3 November 1890, Emanuel Suter Collection, Virginia Mennonite Conference Archives, Eastern Mennonite Univ., Harrisonburg, VA. Hawthorn had also built the kiln for Sherratt's Virginia Pottery Company. See Suter, "'Unless Delayed.'"

42. Emanuel Suter Diary, 5 February 1891, Emanuel Suter Collection, Virginia Mennonite Conference Archives, Eastern Mennonite Univ., Harrisonburg, VA.

43. Richard D. La Guardia, *A History of Trenton 1679–1929* (Trenton, NJ: Trenton Historical Society, 1929).

44. Although Hawthorn's design was not patented until 1894, he would most likely have been building and testing his model before the patent was issued.

45. Patent No. 515,221, United States Patent Office, 20 February 1894.

46. Ibid.

47. Emanuel Suter Diary, 13 November and 19 November, 1891, Emanuel Suter Collection, Virginia Mennonite Conference Archives, Eastern Mennonite Univ., Harrisonburg, VA.

48. "Harrisonburg, Rockingham County, Virginia, 1891," Sanborn Map Company, Sanborn-Perris Map Co. Sanborn (Firm), "Sanborn Fire Insurance Maps," (Teaneck, NJ: Chadwyck-Healey, 1983).

49. Memorandum book advertising North-Western Railways, Emanuel Suter Collection, Virginia Mennonite Conference Archives, Eastern Mennonite Univ., Harrisonburg, VA. A number of small advertising memo books are collected in the Suter papers. It appears that Suter usually carried one of these in his pocket for jotting down ideas, measurements, notes, and even grocery lists when necessary.

50. F. H. Cowden offered Suter the following advice concerning kiln size: "A kiln about 29 ft. long and 14 ft. wide outside will hold 4,000 gal. setting as loose as I do. I saw a kiln about the size of mine in [illegible] New York the other week and the owner of the pottery says it will hold 10,000 gals. It was 19 ft in diameter, a round kiln." Cowden to Emanuel Suter, 6 September 1890, Harrisburg, PA, Emanuel Suter Collection, Virginia Mennonite Conference Archives, Eastern Mennonite Univ., Harrisonburg, VA.

51. Emanuel Suter to Margaret Suter, 24 November 1890, Emanuel Suter Collection, Virginia Mennonite Conference Archives, Eastern Mennonite Univ., Harrisonburg, VA.

52. Quoted in Marc Jeffrey Stern, "The Potters of Trenton, New Jersey, 1850–1902: A Study in the Industrialization of Skilled Trades" (Ph.D diss., State Univ. of New York at Stony Brook, 1986), 228.

53. Emanuel Suter Diary, 29 June 1891, Emanuel Suter Collection, Virginia Mennonite Conference Archives, Eastern Mennonite Univ., Harrisonburg, VA. It is curious that Suter would have burned earthenware in this kiln since he seemed to consider the Harrisonburg Steam Pottery a stoneware factory. A week later (7 July 1891) when the first stoneware kiln was opened, Suter made no comment on the quality of the ware.

54. F. H. Cowden to Emanuel Suter, 30 June 1891, Harrisburg, PA, Emanuel Suter Collection, Virginia Mennonite Conference Archives, Eastern Mennonite Univ., Harrisonburg, VA.

55. F. H. Cowden to Emanuel Suter, 3 July 1891, Harrisburg, PA, Emanuel Suter Collection, Virginia Mennonite Conference Archives, Eastern Mennonite Univ., Harrisonburg, VA.

56. F. H. Cowden to Emanuel Suter, 26 July 1891, Harrisburg, PA, Emanuel Suter Collection, Virginia Mennonite Conference Archives, Eastern Mennonite Univ., Harrisonburg, VA.

57. Georgeanna H. Greer, *American Stonewares, The Art and Craft of Utilitarian Potters* (Exton, PA: Schiffer Publishing, 1981), 51.

58. F. H. Cowden to Emanuel Suter, 29 September 1890, Emanuel Suter Collection, Virginia Mennonite Conference Archives, Eastern Mennonite Univ., Harrisonburg, VA.

59. Emanuel Suter Diary, 5 January 1893, Emanuel Suter Collection, Virginia Mennonite Conference Archives, Eastern Mennonite Univ., Harrisonburg, VA.

60. Ibid., 16 March 1893 .

61. Clinton Coffman, interview by Elmer Smith and John Stewart, 11 October 1963, Elmer Smith Collection, Tape # ES-68, Blue Ridge Heritage Archive, Ferrum College, Ferrum, VA.

62. See Greer, *American Stonewares*, 51 and 69.

63. Emanuel Suter Diary, 11 January 1893, Emanuel Suter Collection, Virginia Mennonite Conference Archives, Eastern Mennonite Univ., Harrisonburg, VA.

64. Ibid., 7 June 1894.

65. One business letterhead for the company, however, identifies its products as "Stoneware, Earthenware, Stove Flues, &c."

66. "Affairs of the Land and Improvement Co. during the Past Twelve Months," *Rockingham Register* (Harrisonburg, VA), June 5, 1891.

67. Emanuel Suter Diary, 13 April and 21 May 1891, Emanuel Suter Collection, Virginia Mennonite Conference Archives, Eastern Mennonite Univ., Harrisonburg, VA.

68. Ibid., 18 June 1891.

69. Ibid., 29 June 1891.

70. Ibid., 18 July 1891.

71. Ibid., 16 August 1895.

72. Ibid., 11 January 1893.

73. Perry G. Suter to Emanuel Suter, 17 October 1893, Emanuel Suter Collection, Virginia Mennonite Conference Archives, Eastern Mennonite Univ., Harrisonburg, VA.

74. Edward Herring to Emanuel Suter, 2 December 1895, Emanuel Suter Collection, Virginia Mennonite Conference Archives, Eastern Mennonite Univ., Harrisonburg, VA.

75. Receipt and letter, Charles H. Torsch to Emanuel Suter, 19 April 1895, and Emanuel Suter Diary, 22 April 1895, Emanuel Suter Collection, Virginia Mennonite Conference Archives, Eastern Mennonite Univ., Harrisonburg, VA.

76. Emanuel Suter Diary, 18 June 1896, Emanuel Suter Collection, Virginia Mennonite Conference Archives, Eastern Mennonite Univ., Harrisonburg, VA.

77. Cowden wrote: "I mix 25 to 50 percent of Woodbridge clay with Amboy. You can use as much as you please. Woodbridge clay spoils to outside color of the ware more than Amboy but is much safer to burn and cool." F. H. Cowden to Emanuel Suter, 29 September 1890, Harrisburg, PA, Emanuel Suter Collection, Virginia Mennonite Conference Archives, Eastern Mennonite Univ., Harrisonburg, VA.

78. Emanuel Suter Diary, 3 April 1894, Emanuel Suter Collection, Virginia Mennonite Conference Archives, Eastern Mennonite Univ., Harrisonburg, VA.

79. Rose & Son business card, Emanuel Suter Collection, Virginia Mennonite Conference Archives, Eastern Mennonite Univ., Harrisonburg, VA.

80. See diary entry for 6 April 1894 and a letter written by Emanuel Suter to his wife, Elizabeth, also dated 6 April 1894. He wrote to Elizabeth: "I seen wonderful things to day. I walked across the brooklyn bridge & rode back on the R. R. Seen the Tower of Liberty[,] was up in the tower of the worlds building the whole of New York & Brooklyn & Jersey cities lay before me, also Statan [sic] govern [Governors] & Coonie [Coney] Islands. Seen vessels of every description in every direction plowing the deep waters of the Beas [East?] & Hudson River." Emanuel Suter Collection, Virginia Mennonite Conference Archives, Eastern Mennonite Univ., Harrisonburg, VA.

81. F. H. Cowden to Emanuel Suter, 8 April 1891, Harrisburg, PA, Emanuel Suter Collection, Virginia Mennonite Conference Archives, Eastern Mennonite Univ., Harrisonburg, VA. Suter had visited Ernst and Furman in 1890.

82. W. S. Coffman to Emanuel Suter, 9 April 1895, Mt. Hermon, Rockingham County, VA, Emanuel Suter Collection, Virginia Mennonite Conference Archives, Eastern Mennonite Univ., Harrisonburg, VA.

83. Emanuel Suter Diary, 6 April 1894, Emanuel Suter Collection, Virginia Mennonite Conference Archives, Eastern Mennonite Univ., Harrisonburg, VA. In January of 1895 Suter recorded: "The boys went with a load of straw to load a car load of ware for Smith of New York." Since this is eight months after the original order was placed, it seems reasonable that this load may have been in response to a subsequent order, indicating a lasting business relationship between Suter and this New York merchant. Emanuel Suter Diary, 15 January 1895, Emanuel Suter Collection, Virginia Mennonite Conference Archives, Eastern Mennonite Univ., Harrisonburg, VA.

84. Emanuel Suter Diary, 9 April 1894, Emanuel Suter Collection, Virginia Mennonite Conference Archives, Eastern Mennonite Univ., Harrisonburg, VA.

85. Ibid., 5 June 1894.

86. Ibid., 7 June 1894; see also diary entry for 6 June 1894.

87. Ibid., 12 February 1895.

88. Ibid., 26 November 1891.

89. Ibid., 15 June 1891.

90. F. H. Cowden to Emanuel Suter, 6 September 1890, Harrisburg, PA, Emanuel Suter Collection, Virginia Mennonite Conference Archives, Eastern Mennonite Univ., Harrisonburg, VA.

91. Phil Schaltenbrand, *Big Ware Turners: The History and Manufacture of Pennsylvania Stoneware, 1720–1920* (Bentleyville, PA: Westerwald Press, 2002), 54. Initially working with John Young at Willson's & Young pottery, Shem Thomas and Young formed their own business in 1856. After this short-lived venture, Thomas worked for John Wallace Cowden, who founded his own pottery after purchasing the Willson's business in 1861. Cowden's firm became Cowden and Wilcox in 1863 when potter Isaac Wilcox joined the business; thus, forming the company to which Emanuel Suter was drawn in 1865. See also Matthew R. Miller, *Decorated Stoneware of Cowden and the Stoneware Potteries of Harrisburg, Pennsylvania, 1852–1924* (Sherman Dale, PA: privately printed, 2001).

92. Perry G. Suter to Emanuel Suter, 20 October 1892, Emanuel Suter Collection, Virginia Mennonite Conference Archives, Eastern Mennonite Univ., Harrisonburg, VA.

93. Emanuel Suter Diary, 2 January 1897, Emanuel Suter Collection, Virginia Mennonite Conference Archives, Eastern Mennonite Univ., Harrisonburg, VA.

94. F. H. Cowden to Emanuel Suter, 29 September 1890, Emanuel Suter Collection, Virginia Mennonite Conference Archives, Eastern Mennonite Univ., Harrisonburg, VA.

95. Isaac Good, Account Book, 66–67.

96. Comstock, *The Pottery of the Shenandoah Region*, 392 and 479.

97. See Emanuel Suter, Account Book, Emanuel Suter Collection, Virginia Mennonite Conference Archives, Eastern Mennonite Univ., Harrisonburg, VA. On page 173 Suter recorded the types, number of gallons, and size of ware he turned for the Harrisonburg Steam Pottery in 1893. It represents a substantial output.

98. Emanuel Suter Diary, 17 August 1895, Emanuel Suter Collection, Virginia Mennonite Conference Archives, Eastern Mennonite Univ., Harrisonburg, VA.

99. Ibid., 10 April 1897.

100. See Kaufman, *Heatwole and Suter Pottery*, 12, and Paul R. Mullins, "Traditional Pottery Adaptation in the Shenandoah Valley: The Diaries and Business Records of Emanuel Suter" delivered at the Council for Northeast Archaeology, 1989, TMs [photocopy], 10, Emanuel Suter Collection, Virginia Mennonite Conference Archives, Eastern Mennonite Univ., Harrisonburg, VA.

101. Emanuel Suter Diary, 1 March 1899, Emanuel Suter Collection, Virginia Mennonite Conference Archives, Eastern Mennonite Univ., Harrisonburg, VA.

102. *Rockingham Register*, October 17, 1902.

103. Rockingham County (VA) Deed Book 79, page 296.

Epilogue

1. See Suter, "'Unless Delayed by Unforeseen Circumstances.'"

2. D. W. Meinig, *The Shaping of America: A Geographical Perspective on 500 Years of History*, vol. 2, *Continental America, 1800–1867* (New Haven: Yale Univ. Press, 1993), 391.

3. For a look at how Harrisonburg evolved after 1900 see Scott Hamilton Suter and David Ehrenpreis, "Boosterism and Heritage: Postcards of Harrisonburg, 1900–1915," David Ehrenpreis ed., in *Picturing Harrisonburg: Visions of a Shenandoah Valley City Since 1828* (Staunton, VA: George F. Thompson Publishing, 2017), 89–118.

4. *The Old Commonwealth* (Harrisonburg, VA), 22 November 1865.

5. Comstock, *The Pottery of the Shenandoah Valley Region*, 419.

6. See Evans and Suter, *"A Great Deal of Stone and Earthenware,"* 27–28.

BIBLIOGRAPHY

Primary Sources

Manuscripts

Good, Isaac. Account Books. Private collection, Harrisonburg, VA. Copy in the Menno Simons
   Historical Library and Archives, Eastern Mennonite University, Harrisonburg, VA.

Suter, Emanuel. Account Books and Business Papers. The Archives of the Virginia Mennonite
   Conference, Harrisonburg, VA.

———. Diaries, 1864–1902. The Archives of the Virginia Mennonite Conference, Harrisonburg,
   VA.

———. Personal and Business Letters. The Archives of the Virginia Mennonite Conference,
   Harrisonburg, VA.

Suter, Mary E. *Explanatory Notes on the Emanuel Suter Diaries, 1864–1902.* The Archives of the
   Virginia Mennonite Conference, Harrisonburg, VA.

Interviews

Coffman, Clinton. Interview by Elmer Smith, October 1963. Blue Ridge Institute, Ferrum
   College, Ferrum, VA.

Grove, Grace Suter. Interview by author, 3 August 1992.

Horst, Orpha. Interview by author, 7 June 1990.

Lindsey, Mary. Interview by author, 20 May 1993.

Suter, Alice Heatwole. Interview by author, 3 August 1992.

Suter, Eugene. Interview by Elmer Smith and John Stewart, July 1963. Blue Ridge Institute,
   Ferrum College, Ferrum, VA.

Suter, Mary E. Interview by author, 10 March 1986.

Secondary Sources

Adams, Henry. *The Education of Henry Adams.* Boston: Privately Printed, 1907. Reprinted New
   York: Literary Classics of the United States, 1983.

Ayers, Edward L. *The Promise of the New South: Life after Reconstruction.* New York: Oxford
   University Press, 1992.

Ayers, Edward L., and John C. Willis, eds. *The Edge of the South.* Charlottesville: University
   Press of Virginia, 1991.

Bender, Harold, et al. *The Mennonite Encyclopedia: A Comprehensive Reference Work on the Anabaptist Mennonite Movement.* Scottdale, PA: Mennonite Publishing House, 1959.

Binns, Charles F. *The Story of the Potter*. London: George Newnes, Limited, 1898.

Bivins, John F., Jr. "The Moravian Potters in North Carolina, 1756–1821." In *Ceramics in America*, edited by Ian M.G. Quimby, 255–90. Charlottesville: University of Virginia Press, 1973.

———. *The Moravian Potters in North Carolina*. Chapel Hill: University of North Carolina Press, 1972.

Borie, Beauveau, IV. *Farming and Folk Society Threshing Among the Pennsylvania Germans*. Ann Arbor: UMI Research Press, 1986.

Bowman, Carl F. *Brethren Society: The Cultural Transformation of a "Peculiar People."* Baltimore: Johns Hopkins University Press, 1995.

Branin, M. Lelyn. *The Early Makers of Handcrafted Earthenware and Stoneware in Central and Southern New Jersey*. Rutherford, NJ: Fairleigh Dickinson University Press, 1988.

Bronner, Simon J., and Joshua R. Brown, eds. *Pennsylvania Germans: An Interpretive Encyclopedia*. Baltimore: Johns Hopkins University Press, 2017.

Brunk, Harry Anthony. *David Heatwole and His Descendants*. Harrisonburg, VA: Park View Press, 1987.

———. *History of Mennonites in Virginia, 1727–1900*. Vol. 1. Staunton, VA: McClure Printing Co., 1959.

Burrison, John A. *Brothers in Clay: The Story of Georgia Folk Pottery*. Athens: University of Georgia Press, 1983.

Bushman, Richard L. *The Refinement of America: Persons, Houses, Cities*. New York: Alfred A. Knopf, 1992.

Carr, Minnie R. "'Potter' John Heatwole." *The Valley Mennonite Register* 5, nos. 27–29 (January 1967).

Carver, Craig M. *American Regional Dialects: A Word Geography*. Ann Arbor: University of Michigan Press, 1987.

Chappell, Edward A. "Cultural Change in the Shenandoah Valley: Northern Augusta County Houses before 1861." Master's thesis, University of Virginia, 1977.

Comstock, H. E. Introduction to *Folk Pottery of the Shenandoah Valley*, by William E. Wiltshire, III, 9–23. New York: E. P. Dutton, 1975.

———. *The Pottery of the Shenandoah Valley Region*. Winston-Salem, NC: The Museum of Early Southern Decorative Arts, 1994.

Conzen, Michael. "Ethnicity on the Land." In *The Making of the American Landscape*, edited by Michael Conzen, 221–48. London: HarperCollins Academic, 1990.

Custer, Milo. *The Reverend Alexander Miller of Virginia and Some of His Descendants*. Bloomington, IL: s.n., 1910.

Danbom, David B. *Born in the Country: A History of Rural America*. Baltimore: Johns Hopkins University Press, 1995.

Dobson, Edward. *A Rudimentary Treatise on the Manufacture of Bricks and Tiles containing an Outline of the Principles of Brickmaking*. 11th ed. London: Crosby Lockwood and Son, 1903.

Ensminger, Robert F. *The Pennsylvania Barn: Its Origin, Evolution, and Distribution in North America*. Baltimore: Johns Hopkins University Press, 1992.

Evans, Jeffrey S., and Scott Hamilton Suter. *"A Great Deal of Stone & Earthenware": The Rockingham County, Virginia School of Folk Pottery*. Dayton, VA: Harrisonburg-Rockingham Historical Society, 2004.

Everhart, J. Otis. *Drain Tile Manufactured in Ohio*. The Engineering Experiment Station, Bulletin No. 51. Columbus: Ohio State University, 1929.

Fanelli, Doris Devine. "John H. Sonner's Stoneware Pottery, Strasburg, Virginia." *Spinning Wheel* (January–February 1981): 42–46.

Gates, William C., Jr. *The City of Hills and Kilns: Life and Work in East Liverpool, Ohio*. East Liverpool: East Liverpool Historical Society, 1984.

Glass, Joseph W. *The Pennsylvania Culture Region: A View from the Barn*. Ann Arbor: UMI Research Press, 1986.

Glassie, Henry. *Pattern in the Material Folk Culture of the Eastern United States*. Philadelphia: University of Pennsylvania Press, 1968.

Good, E. Richard. *Enlarging the Borders: Virginia Mennonite Conference, 150 Years of Expansion*. Harrisonburg, VA: Virginia Mennonite Conference, 1985.

Greer, Georgeanna H. *American Stonewares, The Art and Craft of Utilitarian Potters*. Exton, PA: Schiffer Publishing, 1981.

Hartzler, J. S., and Daniel Kauffman. *Mennonite Church History*. Scottdale, PA: Mennonite Book and Tract Society, 1905.

Heatwole, John L. *The Burning: Sheridan's Devastation of the Shenandoah Valley*. Berryville, VA: Rockbridge Publishing, 1998.

Heatwole, L. J. "A Sketch of the Life and Work of Emanuel Suter." *Mennonite Yearbook and Directory* (1906): 31–32.

Hofstra, Warren R. and Karl Raitz, eds. *The Great Valley Road of Virginia: Shenandoah Landscapes from Prehistory to the Present*. Charlottesville: University of Virginia Press, 2010.

Horne, Catherine Wilson, ed. *Crossroads of Clay: The Southern Alkaline-Glazed Stoneware Tradition*. Columbia: McKissick Museum, 1990.

Horst, Samuel. *Mennonites in the Confederacy: A Study in Civil War Pacifism*. Scottdale, PA: Herald Press, 1967.

Hounshell, David A. *From the American System to Mass Production, 1800–1932: The Development of Manufacturing Technology in the United States*. Baltimore: Johns Hopkins University Press, 1984.

James, Arthur E. *The Potters and Potteries of Chester County, Pennsylvania*. 2nd ed. Exton, PA: Schiffer Publishing Ltd., 1978.

Jordan, Terry G. "The Concept and Method." In *Regional Studies: The Interplay of Land and People*, ed. Glen Lich, 8–24. College Station: Texas A & M University Press, 1992.

Kaufman, Stanley A. *Heatwole and Suter Pottery*. Harrisonburg: Good Printers, 1978.

Keim, Albert N., ed. *The Mennonite Experience in America*. Scottdale, PA: Herald Press, 1985.

Ketchum, William C., Jr. *Potters and Potteries of New York State, 1650–1900*. 2nd ed. Syracuse: Syracuse University Press, 1987.

Koons, Kenneth E. "'The Staple of Our Country': Wheat in the Regional Farm Economy of the Nineteenth-Century Valley of Virginia." In *After the Backcountry: Rural Life in the*

Great Valley of Virginia, 1800–1900, edited by Koons and Warren Hofstra, 3–20. Knoxville: University of Tennessee Press, 2000.

Koons, Kenneth E., and Warren R Hofstra. *After the Backcountry : Rural Life in the Great Valley of Virginia, 1800–1900*. Knoxville: University of Tennessee Press, 2000.

Kouwenhoven, John A. *The Arts in Modern American Civilization*. New York: W. W. Norton, 1948.

Kraybill, Donald B., Steven M. Nolt, and Edsel Burdge, Jr. "Language Use among Anabaptist Groups." In *Pennsylvania Germans: An Interpretive Encyclopedia*, edited by Simon J. Bronner and Joshua R. Brown, 108–30. Baltimore: Johns Hopkins University Press, 2017.

Kurath, Hans. *A Word Geography of the Eastern United States*. Ann Arbor: University of Michigan Press, 1949.

La Guardia, Richard D. *A History of Trenton 1679–1929*. Trenton, NJ: Trenton Historical Society, 1929.

Lasansky, Jeanette. *Made of Mud: Stoneware Potteries in Central Pennsylvania, 1831–1929*. University Park: Pennsylvania State University Press, 1979.

———. *Central Pennsylvania Redware Pottery, 1780–1904*. Lewisburg, PA: Union County Oral Traditions Projects, 1979. Reprinted 1989.

Lehman, James O., and Steven M. Nolt. *Mennonites, Amish, and the American Civil War*. Baltimore: Johns Hopkins University Press, 2007.

Long, Amos, Jr. *The Pennsylvania German Family Farm*. Breinigsville, PA: The Pennsylvania German Society, 1972.

Maas, John. *The Glorious Enterprise: The Centennial Exhibition and H.J. Schwarzmann, Architect-in-Chief*. Watkins Glen, NY: American Life Foundation, 1973.

MacMaster, Richard K. *Land, Piety, Peoplehood: The Establishment of Mennonite Communities in America, 1683–1790*. Scottdale, PA: Herald Press, 1985.

Majewski, John. *A House Dividing: Economic Development in Pennsylvania and Virginia before the Civil War*. New York: Cambridge University Press, 2000.

McCormick, Cyrus. *The Century of the Reaper*. Boston: Houghton, Mifflin Co., 1931.

McMurry, Sally. *Families and Farmhouses in Nineteenth-Century America: Vernacular Design and Social Change*. Knoxville: University of Tennessee Press, 1997.

———. "Who Read the Agricultural Journals? Evidence from Chenango County, New York, 1839–1865." *Agricultural History* 63 (Fall 1989): 1–19.

Meinig, D. W. *Atlantic America, 1492–1800*. Vol. 1 of *The Shaping of America: A Geographical Perspective on 500 Years of History*. New Haven: Yale University Press, 1986.

———. *Continental America, 1800–1867*. Vol 2 of *The Shaping of America: A Geographical Perspective on 500 Years of History*. New Haven: Yale University Press, 1993.

Miller, Matthew R. *Decorated Stoneware of Cowden and the Stoneware Potteries of Harrisburg Pennsylvania, 1852–1924*. Shermans Dale, PA: Matthew R. Miller, 2001.

Miller, Merritt Finley. T*he Evolution of Reaping Machines*. United States Department of Agriculture, Farmer's Bulletin No. 103. Washington, DC: Government Printing Office, 1902.

Mitchell, Robert D. *Commercialism and Frontier: Perspectives on the Early Shenandoah Valley*. Charlottesville: University of Virginia Press, 1977.

Mullins, Paul R. "Traditional Pottery Adaptation in the Shenandoah Valley: The Diaries and Business Records of Emanuel Suter." Presentation at the Council for Northeast Archaeology, 1989, TMs [photocopy]. Menno Simons Historical Library and Archives, Eastern Mennonite University, Harrisonburg, VA.

Myers, Susan. *Handcraft to Industry: Philadelphia Ceramics in the First Half of the Nineteenth Century.* Smithsonian Studies in History and Technology, no. 43. Washington, DC: Smithsonian Institution Press, 1980.

Powell, Elizabeth *A. Pennsylvania Pottery: Tools and Processes.* Doylestown, PA: Bucks County Historical Society, 1972.

Randel, William Peirce. *Centennial: American Life in 1876.* Philadelphia: Chilton Book Co., 1969.

Rasmussen, Wayne D. "The Civil War: A Catalyst of Agricultural Revolution." *Agricultural History* 39 (October 1965): 187–95.

———. "The Impact of Technological Change on American Agriculture, 1862–1962." *Journal of Economic History* 20 (December 1962): 578–91.

Redekop, Calvin. *Mennonite Society.* Baltimore: Johns Hopkins University Press, 1989.

Rhodes, Daniel. *Clay and Glazes for the Potter.* Philadelphia: Chilton Book Co., 1957.

Rice, A. H., and John Baer Stoudt. *The Shenandoah Pottery.* Strasburg, VA: printed by the authors, 1929. Reprinted Berryville, VA: Virginia Book Co., 1974.

Rinzler, Ralph, and Robert Sayers. *The Meaders Family: North Georgia Potters.* Smithsonian Folklife Studies, no. 1. Washington, DC: Smithsonian Institution Press, 1980.

Rodes, David S, and Norman R. Wenger. *Unionists and the Civil War Experience in the Shenandoah Valley.* Vol. 3, edited by Emmert F. Bittinger. Dayton, VA: Valley Research Associates and Valley Brethren-Mennonite Heritage Center, 2005.

Rydell, Robert W. *All the World's a Fair: Visions of Empire at American International Expositions, 1876–1916.* Chicago: University of Chicago Press, 1984.

Sappington, Roger E. *The Brethren in Virginia.* Harrisonburg, VA: Park View Press, 1973.

Schaltenbrand, Phil. *Big Ware Turners: The History and Manufacture of Pennsylvania Stoneware, 1720–1920.* Bentleyville, PA: Westerwald Publishing, 2002.

———. *Old Pots: Salt-Glazed Stoneware of the Greensboro-New Geneva Region.* Hanover, PA: Everybody's Press, 1977.

Schlabach, Theron F. *Peace, Faith, Nation: Mennonites and Amish in Nineteenth-Century America.* Scottdale, PA: Herald Press, 1985.

Schlebecker, John T. *Whereby We Thrive: A History of American Farming, 1607–1972.* Ames: Iowa State University Press, 1975.

Smith, Elmer Lewis, John G. Stewart, and M. Ellsworth Kyger. *The Pennsylvania Germans of the Shenandoah Valley.* Allentown, PA: Schlechter's, 1964.

Stachiw, Myron, and Nora Pat Small. "Tradition and Transformation: Rural Society and Architectural Change in Nineteenth-century Central Massachusetts." In *Perspectives in Vernacular Architecture.* Vol. 3, edited by Thomas Carter and Bernard L. Herman. Columbia: University of Missouri Press, 1989.

Stern, Marc Jeffrey. *The Pottery Industry of Trenton: A Skilled Trade in Transition, 1850–1929.* New Brunswick, NJ: Rutgers University Press, 1994.

Suter, Marian B., ed. *More Memories of Yesteryear: An Updated Genealogy of the Family of Daniel Suter (1808–1873)*. Harrisonburg, VA: Campbell, 2017.

Suter, Mary, and Grace Grove. *Keepers of the Spring: A History of Little North Mountain Sparkling Springs*. Harrisonburg, VA: printed by the authors, 1987.

Suter, Mary Eugenia. *Memories of Yesteryear: A History of the Suter Family*. Waynesboro, VA: Charles F. McClung, 1959.

Suter, Scott Hamilton, and David Ehrenpreis. "Boosterism and Heritage: Postcards of Harrisonburg, 1900–1915." In *Picturing Harrisonburg: Visions of a Shenandoah Valley City Since 1828*, edited by David Ehrenpreis, 89–118. Staunton, VA: George F. Thompson Publishing, 2017.

———. "Otto Karle: A Previously Unknown Shenandoah Valley Potter." In *Ceramics in America 2005*, edited by Robert Hunter, 229–32. Milwaukee: Chipstone Foundation, 2005.

———. *Shenandoah Valley Folklife*. Jackson: University Press of Mississippi, 1999.

———. "'Unless Delayed by Unforeseen Circumstances': A Tale of a Shenandoah Valley Industrial Pottery." In *Ceramics in America 2018*, edited by Robert Hunter. Milwaukee: Chipstone Foundation, 2018.

Sweet, Palmer C. *Virginia Clay Material Resources*. Charlottesville: Virginia Department of Conservation and Economic Development, Division of Mineral Resources, 1982. Publication 36.

Sweezy, Nancy. *Raised in Clay: The Southern Pottery Tradition*. Washington, DC: Smithsonian Institution Press, 1984.

Taveau, Augustin L. "Modern Farming in America." In *Report of the Commissioner of Agriculture for 1874*. Washington, D C: Government Printing Office, 1875.

Truman, Benjamin. *History of the World's Fair Being a Complete and Authentic Description of the Columbian Exposition from its Inception*. Philadelphia: Syndicate Publishing, 1893.

Turnbaugh, Sarah Peabody, ed. *Domestic Pottery in the North East United States, 1625–1850*. Orlando: Academic Press, 1985.

US Department of Agriculture. *Bibliography on Soil Erosion and Soil and Water Conservation*. Miscellaneous Publication No. 312. Washington, DC: Government Printing Office, 1938.

Wayland, John W. *A History of Rockingham County, Virginia*. Dayton, VA: Ruebush-Elkins Co., 1912. Reprinted Harrisonburg, VA: C. J. Carrier Co., 1980.

Wenger, J. C. *The Mennonite Church in America*. Scottdale, PA: Herald Press, 1966.

Whipp, Richard. *Patterns of Labour: Work and Social Change in the Pottery Industry*. New York: Routledge, 1990.

Willet, E. Henry, and Joey Brackner. *The Traditional Pottery of Alabama*. Montgomery: Montgomery Museum of Fine Arts, 1983.

Wust, Klaus. *The Virginia Germans*. Charlottesville: University of Virginia Press, 1969.

Wynes, Charles E., ed. *Southern Sketches from Virginia, 1881–1901*. Charlottesville: University of Virginia Press, 1964.

Zigler, D. H. *A History of the Brethren in Virginia*. Elgin, IL: Brethren Publishing House, 1908.

Zug, Charles G., III. *Turners and Burners: The Folk Potters of North Carolina*. The Fred W. Morrison Series in Southern Studies. Chapel Hill: University of North Carolina Press, 1986.